Become Fluent in the Lost Language of the Tree Ogham

Establish a close bond and communion with the twenty magical trees of the Celtic Tree Ogham. As living, growing aspects of the Green World, the trees reveal their ancient spiritual wisdom and magical secrets to those who learn to decipher their messages. With the insight and direction in *Celtic Tree Mysteries*, you can become fluent in the secret language of the Tree Ogham.

Written by a recognized authority on Celtic spirituality and magic, this trusted reference manual will guide you along the Green World path of self-transformation, magical development, and spiritual growth.

About the Author

Steve Blamires was born in Ayr, Scotland, in 1955, and currently lives in Alaska. At the age of nineteen, he began his studies with Gareth Knight and the legendary Company of Hawkwood. After studying the Western Mystery Tradition for twelve years, his interest moved to his Celtic roots. Ever since, he has concentrated on promoting all facets of this ancient tradition.

In 1986, Mr. Blamires founded the Celtic Research and Folklore Society (CRFS) as a way of helping others along the Celtic path. He has produced many magazine articles for several publications in the U.K. and the U.S.A.; writes and edits the CRFS journal, *Seanchas*; and carries out research on behalf of other authors and groups. He gives talks throughout the U.K. and U.S.A. on Celtic spirituality and magic, and carries on the ancient tradition of storytelling. In Chicago, Mr. Blamires represented the interests of the indigenous Celtic peoples at the Council for a Parliament of the World's Religions. He has most recently been working with Tibetan Buddhist monks to make Holy Isle, Scotland, a place of spiritual retreat for people of all beliefs.

To Write to the Author

If you wish to contact the author or would like more information about this book, please write to the author in care of Llewellyn Worldwide and we will forward your request. Both the author and publisher appreciate hearing from you and learning of your enjoyment of this book. Llewellyn Worldwide cannot guarantee that every letter written to the author will be answered, but all will be forwarded. Please write to:

Steve Blamires
℅ Llewellyn Worldwide
P.O. Box 64383, Dept. K070–1
St. Paul, MN 55164-0383, U.S.A.

Please enclose a self-addressed stamped envelope for reply, or $1.00 to cover costs. If outside U.S.A., enclose international postal reply coupon.

Celtic Tree

mysteries

Practical Druid Magic & Divination

Steve Blamires

2002
Llewellyn Publications
St. Paul, Minnesota 55164-0383

FIRST EDITION
Fourth Printing, 2002

Cover Design: Gavin Dayton Duffy
    Tree roots photo © Photodisc
Illustrations: Nicola Jane Swinton
Editing and Layout: Designed to Sell
Project Coordinators: Jessica Thoreson and Rebecca Zins

Excerpts from *Cath Maige Tuired*, translated by E. A. Gray (copyright 1983) and "The Frenzy of Mad Sweeney" (copyright 1913) are reprinted by permission of the Irish Texts Society.

Library of Congress Cataloging-in-Publication Data
Blamires, Steve
        Celtic Tree Mysteries: Secrets of the Ogham/Steve
        Blamires.—1st ed.

            p. cm. — (Llewellyn's Celtic Wisdom Series)
        Includes bibliographical references and index.
        Discography: p.
        ISBN 1-56718-070-1 (pbk.)
        1. Magic, Celtic. 2. Tree worship. 3. Ogham alphabet.
    4. Mythology, Celtic. I. Title. II. Series.
    BF1622.C45B55 1997
    133.4'3'089916—dc21   96–36866
                                                                  CIP

Llewellyn Worldwide does not participate in, endorse, or have any authority or responsibility concerning private business transactions between our authors and the public.
    All mail addressed to the author is forwarded but the publisher cannot, unless specifically instructed by the author, give out an address or phone number.

Llewellyn Publications
A Division of Llewellyn Worldwide, Ltd.
St. Paul, Minnesota 55164-0383, U.S.A.
www.llewellyn.worldwide

Printed in the United States of America

Other Books by the Author

Glamoury: Magic of the Celtic Green World
(Llewellyn Publications, 1995)

The Irish Celtic Magical Tradition
(The Aquarian Press, 1992)

Other Writings

Seanchas: Journal of the Celtic Research and Folklore Society
Published quarterly since 1986.

For Helen of the Golden Hair —
dream, my lovely, dream.

CONTENTS

Contents

PART THREE

ACKNOWLEDGMENTS

The writing of this book was a long and difficult process, and certainly not an easy task for me. I would like to express my sincere gratitude to those who helped me along the way, and who encouraged me and picked me up when I was down. In particular, I wish to thank all my good friends in Eamhain Abhlach, and especially Nikkii for providing the excellent illustrations which have so beautifully made the trees come to life on the page. I also wish to express my sincere thanks to the Irish Texts Society, who have allowed me to quote so extensively from their excellent translations of the Irish legends.

Above all my most sincere thanks and love go to my beautiful Helen, a constant inspiration to me, a true, dear friend and partner.

INTRODUCTION

This book is a detailed examination of the Tree Alphabet, one of the most misunderstood of the various forms of practical magic. I also consider the equally misunderstood Ogham script, which is often equated with the older Tree Alphabet. My intent is to show that these are in fact two separate systems, although they can be combined for magical purposes. More than an academic discussion, this book is a practical manual detailing useful and workable information about trees, tree magic, and personal spiritual development.

Magic—any form of magic—brings about changes not only in the physical world, but also in the spiritual aspect of the magician. This simple fact is often overlooked, or perhaps misunderstood by many who claim to perform magic. According to the Celtic tradition, the physical level and the spiritual level are inextricably linked; you cannot affect one without affecting the other. It is for this reason that I place a great deal of emphasis on the spiritual development of the magician. Keep this in mind as you attempt the Practical Work, and by the end of the book, you should have enough of a grounding in this ancient form of magic to make successful use of it in your day-to-day life, and to bring about progress and development on your spiritual level.

Trees are living, changing entities in the Green World, and so, too, is the magic associated with them. What follows in this book is a system which has been developed and adapted over centuries to the changes in society. As presented here, it is suited to our modern lifestyle, and is not an attempt to recreate a system which has long since ceased to be of relevance.

It could be said that the only thing which has remained constant since the days of the ancient Irish druids are the trees themselves. This is why I have devoted a certain amount of space to the examination of the physical trees. Most readers have seen many different kinds of trees, can name several of them, and can even identify them by their bark or grain patterns. These are useful abilities which will enhance your understanding of higher aspects of trees, much of which you may not yet be aware. The life forms of the Green World have a great deal to teach us, too much of which has been forgotten over the centuries as we cut ourselves off from the forces around and within us. I hope that together we may go some way toward redressing this imbalance.

PART ONE

CHAPTER ONE

THE ORIGINS OF OGHAM

Those of you already familiar with Celtic magical tradition may be surprised to see that I discuss Ogham script and the Tree Alphabet separately, rather than treat them as one subject as is usually the case. I shall explain my reasons for this in detail later in the book. For now, here is an overview of Ogham: when it was used, how it was used, and what we know about it. There is often confusion and disagreement over even these basic topics; however, once you understand them, you can go on to an examination of the more esoteric uses of Ogham and its connection to the Tree Alphabet.

Ogham (oh-am) script most often takes the form of a series of notches or lines, known as *flesc* (flayshk), which are spaced along a central stem-line and carved into a standing stone. These stones are found throughout Ireland and the British Isles, and contain the best examples of this method of writing. The letters themselves are called *feda* (fay-dah) and the consonants are referred to as *taebomnai* (tay-bow-nih). There is another group of letters known as the *forfeda* (fore-fay-dah), or supplementary characters, which are identified in ancient Irish manuscripts on Ogham, but which rarely appear on the standing stones. These characters seem to have been added to the alphabet at a later date, perhaps to make it more consistent with the Greek and Latin alphabets.

These old names for the notches, letters, and consonants are probably the source of the perceived connections between trees and Ogham. The word *flesc* means "twig," *feda* means "wood" or "trees," and *taebomnai* means the "side of the trunk of a tree." As we shall see later, these names have symbolic importance, but do not relate to real, natural trees as does the Tree Ogham.

Ogham script does not appear to have developed out of any earlier form of writing, but is as if one individual thought out the entire system. This is not as unlikely as it may first appear. The development of Ogham in Ireland was contemporaneous with the introduction of Latin and the Roman alphabet for ecclesiastical use. If Irishmen were learning to write using Latin and the Roman alphabet, perhaps other learned men of the day decided to develop a Celtic form of writing at the same time. The oldest known stone inscriptions are based on the structure of the Latin alphabet, but use the Primitive Irish language. Primitive Irish dates from before the sixth century, whereas all of the known Ogham stones date from between the fifth and seventh centuries, except for some Pictish stones in Scotland, which may be from as late as the ninth century. Three hundred thirty-two Irish-language, Ogham-inscribed stones have been discovered in Ireland, most in Munster and areas occupied by the Deise and Laighin tribes. There are forty stones in Wales, some of which repeat the Ogham dedication in the Roman alphabet. These Welsh stones are all in areas inhabited by tribes originally from Ireland. There are eight in England, five in the Isle of Man, and two in Scotland, plus an additional twenty-seven in Scotland inscribed in the Pictish language. These Pictish stones use the same style of Ogham writing, but because we know nothing of the Pictish language, attempts to translate them have proven futile. In recent years, several Ogham stones have been identified in North America, opening a whole new area of research on Celtic migration, which is beyond the scope of this work.

The small number of discovered stones leaves us with few Ogham inscriptions to examine. Because the inscriptions consist of names only, they tell us very little about the grammar and correct use of the script. Therefore, we must rely heavily on other sources for this information, which, fortunately for us, are plentiful.

Much has been written about the origins of Ogham and its possible relation to the Norse and Germanic system of Runes. I personally doubt that Ogham is related to the Runes; the names of the letters are most definitely Irish, and do not appear to have been borrowed from any other language. Much has also been made of the fact that, as a form of writing, Ogham is extremely laborious and not very practical. As to this point, it should be remembered that Ogham was only meant to be used on short inscriptions along the edge of a standing stone. A series of straight lines bisecting or resting upon a straight edge is far easier to carve than curving, circular, or joined lettering. Another unlikely theory is that Ogham was some sort of magical or secret script meant to be seen and used by the Druidic order. These standing stones were clearly meant to be seen and read by all comers. The Welsh stones that repeat the inscriptions in Latin are easy to read and understand.

The primary manuscript sources for information on Ogham are *Auraicept Na nEces* (*The Scholar's Primer*), *De Duilib Feda na Forfid* (*Values of the Forfeda*), and *Lebor Ogam* (*Book of Ogham*). These sources are quoted in the twelfth-century *Book of Leinster*, and in the *Book of Ballymote*, written in 1391. There are also references to Ogham in the *Book of Lecan*, written in 1416 by Gilla Isa Mor Mac Firbis, which also refers to much earlier works. In fact, it is from these ancient books that nearly all references to Ogham have been taken; and these manuscripts were compiled several centuries after Ogham was last used in script.

These sources contain lengthy discourse on Ogham, but nowhere in these books is a magical aspect suggested. They are, instead, detailed and tedious discussions of Irish grammar, spelling, and sentence structure. Knowing that these ancient texts were always written for three levels of interpretation, however, we can derive magical content by reading *between* the lines.[1] For example, the *Book of Ballymote* begins its section on Ogham script with the following paragraph:

> When is the Ogham one? Not hard: the whole of it. When is it two things? Not hard: vowels and consonants. When is it three things? Not hard: vowels, diphthongs and consonants. When is it four? Not hard: the three groups of consonants and the ten principle vowels. When is it five? Not hard: vowels, diphthongs and three groups of consonants. When is it six? Not hard: the three composite letters of the Ogham nG, Sr, Qu. When is it seven? Not hard: the three additions to the Primer, Ho, Forsail and Arnin.[2]

This information was very important for trainee bards and poets, who had to follow very strict rules of grammar and syntax when they composed poems and utterances. These same grammatical rules apply to the magical levels of these poems and utterances, and it is possible

---

[1] Under the Celtic system, everything is believed to exist on three levels—physical, mental, and spiritual. In the case of Ogham, the physical level is the ink on the page or the notch on the stone, the mental is the word or letter that ink or notch makes you think of, and the spiritual level is all the associations that letter or word has when used as part of a system of spiritual development.

[2] Unless otherwise stated, all quotations are from *The Scholar's Primer*, translated by George Calder (Edinburgh: Long, 1917).

to use a sound understanding of Irish Celtic magical techniques to read these deeper meanings and find useful and practical material.

The manuscripts refer to more than one hundred different types of Ogham, each with its unique names and different-shaped notches for the letters. The commonly accepted Ogham character set is shown on the next few pages, along with the alphabet structure. Notice that the structure remains the same in the additional examples shown, even thought the names of the letters change. In fact, the names appear to have been chosen simply because they have the correct first initial. This actually seems to be a way of remembering the letters of each alphabet and the order in which they run. (We use a similar system in our schools, teaching our children the alphabet through associations such as A is for Apple, B is for Ball, C is for Cat.) Is there a magical aspect to the groupings? Perhaps there is; and perhaps they would yield a magical system of their own. I know that the Tree Ogham has a practical purpose in magic, and we shall examine this in detail in Part Two.

There are other Ogham alphabets that use the basic Ogham notches, but which repeat every second letter and the last and first letters, double every consonant and so on, in a bewildering array of permutations. None of these scripts has ever been found on an Ogham stone, however, which implies that they were meant for some other purpose. It is also significant that the Ogham found on the stones differs from the Ogham in the manuscripts. The vowels in the manuscripts are always shown as vertical lines bisecting the main horizontal stem-line, whereas on the stones, vowels are carved as dots along the stem-line. Most stone inscriptions read vertically, starting at the bottom of the stone, working up one edge to the top, and occasionally, back down the other side. Despite the hundred or so different Ogham alphabets, the Ogham script characters shown on page eight are the most used, and the ones found on the standing stones.

THE OGHAM CHARACTERS

B L F S N H D T C Q M G nG St R

A O U E I EA OI UI IO AAEE

TREE OGHAM

GROUP B

B	L	F	S	N
Beithe	Luis	Fern	Sail	Nion

GROUP H

H	D	T	C	Q
hUath	Duir	Tinne	Coll	Queirt

GROUP M

M	G	nG	St	R
Muin	Gort	nGetal	Straiph	Ruis

GROUP A

A	O	U	E	I
Ailm	Onn	Ur	Edhadh	Idhadh

---

3 For easier reading and comparison, the Ogham alphabets are shown horizontally here and throughout the book. The vertical script shown on the first page of each chapter will give you an idea of how the script appears on the standing stones.

River-pool Ogham

Group B

B	L	F	S	N
Berba	Luimnech	Febal	Sinand	Nid N

Group H

H	D	T	C	Q
h'Othain	Derg	Teith	Catt	Qusrat

Group M

M	G	nG	St	R
Muinten	Gabal	nGrian	Srur	Rigi

Group A

A	O	U	E	I
Aru	e'Obul	Uisiu	Erbos	Indiurnn

Color Ogham

Group B

B	L	F	S	N
Ban	Liath	Flann	Sodath	Necht
(white)	(gray)	(red)	(fine colored)	(clear)

Group H

H	D	T	C	Q
Huath	Dub	Temen	Cron	Quair
(terrible)	(black)	(dark gray)	(brown)	(mouse-colored)

Group M

M	G	nG	St	R
mBracht	Gorm	nGlas	Sorcha	Ruadh
(variegated)	(blue)	(green)	(bright)	(red)

Group A

A	O	U	E	I
Alad	Odhar	Usgdha	Erc	Irfind
(piebald)	(dun)	(resinous)	(red)	(very white)

FORTRESS OGHAM

GROUP B

B	L	F	S	N
Bruiden	Lifi	Femin	Seolae	Nemthend

GROUP H

H	D	T	C	Q
h'Ochae	Dindrigh	Temair	Cerae	Quorann

GROUP M

M	G	nG	St	R
Mide	Gabarn	Garmon	Streulae	Roigni

GROUP A

A	O	U	E	I
Ae	Ogba	Uisnech	Emain	Iliu

BIRD OGHAM

GROUP B

B	L	F	S	N
Besan (pheasant)	Lachu (duck)	Faelinn (gull)	Segh (hawk)	Naescu (snipe)

GROUP H

H	D	T	C[4]	Q
Hadaig (night raven)	Droen (wren)	Truiteoc (starling)		Querc (hen)

GROUP M

M	G	nG	St	R
Mintan (titmouse)	Geis (swan)	nGeigh (goose)	Stmolach (thrush)	Rocnat (small rook)

GROUP A

A	O	U	E	I
Aidhircleog (lapwing)	Odoroscrach (scrat)	Uiseoc (lark)	Ela (swan)	Illait (eaglet)

---

[4] The letter C in the Bird Ogham is actually missing from the original source manuscript. We do not know why.

The ancient Celtic people had a sound knowledge of the properties of trees and the powers and energies of the Green World. This knowledge was coupled with the Irish language, emerging as the Tree Ogham. What we accept as one thing—a knowledge of the powers of trees—was originally two very different concepts: one a form of practical magical and spiritual instruction, the other a type of writing and spelling. This is referred to in the *Book of Ballymote*, as given in Calder's *The Scholar's Primer*:

> There are two divisions of the *Beithe Luis Nion*—vowels and consonants. Two kinds are reckoned of them—artificial trees, that is the trees of the Ogham, and the natural trees, that is the trees of the forest.

Beithe Luis Nion is the old name for the Tree Ogham. It is clear from this that a difference was recognized between trees—natural and artificial (which had long been a source of magical energy)—and the Ogham script. A further division is presented in the following passage:

> What is measure with regard to Ogham letters? This is their number, five Oghmic groups, i.e. five men for each group and one up to five for each of them. These are their signs—right of stem, left of stem, athwart of stem, through stem, about stem. Thus is a tree climbed—treading on the root of the tree first, with thy right hand first and thy left hand after, then with the stem, then against it and through it and about it.

The Oghmic groups are the subheadings Group B, Group H, Group M, and Group A. The wording in the *Book of Ballymote* is confusing when it mentions the Oghmic groups. It appears to say there are five, when in fact there are only four, but then explains itself when it points out there are five men (or notches) in each of these four groups. The notches mentioned are the branches of the artificial trees on either side of the central stem, or trunk. The names of the letters represent the natural trees—the great woody plants of the Green World.

The ancient Irish legends, which yield a vast amount of practical magic for those who read them on all three levels, mention Ogham only casually, as though it were of little importance to them. The *Book of Ballymote* has a reference that reads:

> Oghma, much skilled in dialects and poetry, invented
> Ogham for signing secret speech known only to the learned.

Oghma was the *trenfher*, literally "strong man" of the gods and goddesses known as the Tuatha De Danann (too-ah dje dahnahn). His full title was Oghma Grianainech (oh-mah gree-an-aneh), which means "Oghma of the Sun-Like Countenance." Although he is known as the great champion of the Tuatha De Danann, note that the quote contains no mention of his physical prowess, but concentrates on his eloquence instead. Also note that he is credited with inventing Ogham for signing secret *speech* as opposed to writing. The "signing of secret speech" may refer to three types of Ogham mentioned in the *Book of Ballymote* and known as Foot Ogham, Nose Ogham, and Palm of Hand Ogham. The section dealing with Foot Ogham says:

> The fingers of the hand about the shinbone for the letters
> and put them on the right of the shinbone for group B,
> left for group H, athwart for group M, straight across for
> group A.

The Nose and Palm of Hand Oghams repeat this set of instructions, but replace shinbone with nose or palm of hand. To spell out a message, you use one to five fingers to represent notches, and place these fingers across the shinbone, nose, or palm of hand. While this describes a communication system, it is extremely doubtful that such a lengthy and complicated means of signing was ever put into practice, nor would it be of much use to us in our magical Work.

Some sources tell us that messages were written in Ogham on lengths of yew and sent from one person to another. Perhaps this was simply communication; perhaps it was communication in code or for magical purposes. Other sources suggest that these inscribed pieces of yew were used as a means of divination. Cuchulain (koo hoo-lin), the great hero of Ulster, seems to have a particular association with Ogham. Throughout his short life, incidents involving Ogham occur usually as a precursor to important events. For example, while still a boy, he came across an iron ring inscribed in Ogham with the words, "If any man comes on this green and if he is a warrior bearing arms, it is *geis* (taboo) for him to leave without challenge to single combat." Cuchulain ignored this warning and threw the ring into a nearby lake. If Cuchulain was familiar with Ogham script from an early age, then it was not just the druids who wrote and read Ogham. Ogham crops up several times in the warrior's later life, particularly during the *Tain Bo Cuailnge* (toyn bo cooly), the "Cattle Raid of Cooley." In one incident, he halts the advancing armies of Queen Meadhbh (may-ev) of Connacht by placing an Ogham-inscribed wooden ring around a standing stone and forbidding the armies to pass until its meaning is deciphered.

He is later said to have placed a four-branched piece of wood in the middle of a ford, again with an Ogham inscription upon it, which likewise halted the progress of an army until its meaning was understood. Later still, he cut down a whole oak tree and inscribed it with Ogham saying that the army could not advance until a man in a chariot had leapt the fallen tree. These examples strongly suggest a magical side to Ogham, for if these pieces of wood were considered to be ordinary and unimportant, the advancing armies would have tossed them aside and marched on. The fact that they did not, and the fact that they felt compelled to do as the Ogham said, shows the power with which it was regarded.

References to Ogham are found in the vast collections of poems and stories of other great Irish and Scottish heros. For example, when Bran mac Feabhail (bron mak fay-vahl) returned from his epic voyage to the Otherworld, he ordered that all he had seen and experienced be carved in words of Ogham to be remembered by all men before he sailed off into the sunset never to be seen again. In the legend of Etain and Midhir, Dallan the druid uses four Ogham-inscribed rods in a scrying ritual to determine the whereabouts of the missing Etain.

We do not know from the legends which of the hundred or so Oghams was used, and despite these references, the only Ogham inscriptions ever found and translated are on commemorative stones. These inscriptions are personal names of seemingly no magical significance. No human remains have ever been found underneath or near such stones, making it doubtful that they were used to commemorate the dead (although some manuscript authors thought this to be the case). Recent work on the Ogham stones indicates that their original purpose may have been as boundary markers for property. This is supported by a seventh-century Irish law stating that disputes over land ownership could be settled by one party proving that he or she was related to the person named on the Ogham stone situated on that land.

If Ogham was used on strips of yew for magical and divinatory purposes, it is unlikely that such wooden artifacts would have survived. So we are left with only the durable standing stones.[5]

The sources we have suggest that the original Ogham may have been a stylized and formal manner of speech, and not a written language. As mentioned above, the Tuatha De Danann champion Oghma was credited with the invention of Ogham as a form of secret speech. (His name was later associated with the written

---

[5] Having said that, there is one amusing piece of Ogham to be found written in the margin of the manuscript known as *Codex Sangallensis 904* in which the scribe apologizes for his poor work that day due to the effects of a hangover!

script.) The Irish god Oghma has the same function as the Gaulish god Ogmios (oy-mos), whose name has the same root as the word Ogham. The second-century Greek traveler and writer Lucian gives a vivid description of Ogmios from a painting he encountered while traveling in Gaul.

> The Celts call Heracles in the language of their country Ogmios. He is an extremely old man with a bald forehead and his few remaining hairs quite gray; his skin is wrinkled and embrowned by the sun but although he is of this appearance he is nevertheless attired like a Heracles for he has on him the lion's skin, and he has a club in his right hand; he is duly equipped with a quiver and his left hand has a bow stretched out. This old man draws after him a great number of men bound by their ears, and the bonds are slender cords wrought of gold and amber, and although they are dragged on by such weak ties, they never try to run away, nor do they resist or struggle against them. Quite the reverse, they follow with joyful countenance in a merry mood praising him who leads them. The painter pierced the tip of his (Ogmios') tongue and represented the people drawn from it, and the god turns a smiling countenance towards those whom he is leading. Now I stood a long time looking at these things but a certain Celt nearby said, "I will tell you the secret of the painting. We Celts do not consider the power of speech to be Hermes but we represent it by means of Heracles for he is much stronger. Nor should you wonder at his being represented by an old man for the power of words is wont to show its perfection in age. So if this old man Heracles, the power of speech, draws men after him, tied to his tongue by their ears, you have no reason to wonder, as you must be aware of the close connection between the tongue and the ears. In a word we Celts are of the opinion that Heracles himself performed everything by

the power of words. His weapons are his utterances which
are sharp and well aimed, swift to pierce the mind."[6]

From this passage we can see that Ogmios was considered by
the Gauls to be their champion, and that it was not by strength
alone he accomplished his feats, but by the skillful use of words.
The Scottish-Gaelic name for Ogham is *oidheam* (oy-am), which
also means "idea," "notion," or "hint." It is therefore not connected with writing, but rather with mental, abstract concepts. The
name, Ogmios, is also a Scottish-Gaelic word that literally means
"young month." This is the name for the month of June, and can be
associated with sunshine and, therefore, Oghma of the Sun-Like
Countenance. (Its literal meaning, young month, refers to when the
summer was acknowledged as starting at Bealtaine in May, and
June was the first, or youngest, full month after summer commenced.) It is not unreasonable to assume, then, that the Irish
champion Oghma also used speech, as opposed to strength alone, to
maintain his position as champion of the Tuatha De Danann.

The manner of speaking employed by these champions often
took the form of a stylized set of questions and answers. The original spoken Ogham may lie in this particular form of language. An
example of this ritualistic parlance appears in *Cath Maige Tuired*
(kah moy tura), the "Battle of Moytura," in the section where Lugh
asks for admission to Tara, and is questioned by the doorkeeper.[7]

> The doorkeeper then asked of him, "What art do you
> practice? For no one without an art enters Tara."
>
> "Question me," he said, "I am a builder."
>
> The doorkeeper answered, "We do not need you. We
> have a builder already, Luchta mac Luachada."

---

6 T. D. Kendrick, *The Druids* (Largs: Banton Press, 1990).
7 Lugh is one of the more important Celtic gods, and many place names throughout Europe still bear his name. In this particular legend, he is the hero who
   musters the army, trains them, and inspires them to defeat the dreaded Fomhoire.

He said, "Question me, doorkeeper, I am a smith."

The doorkeeper answered him, "We have a smith already, Colum Cualeinech of the three new techniques."

He said, "Question me. I am a champion."

The doorkeeper answered, "We do not need you. We have a champion already, Oghma mac Ethlend."

He said again, "Question me. I am a harper."

"We do not need you. We have a harper already, Abcan mac Bicelmois, whom the men of the three gods chose in the sid mounds."

He said, "Question me. I am a warrior."

The doorkeeper answered, "We do not need you. We have a warrior already, Bresal Etarlam mac Echdach Baethlaim."

Then he said, "Question me, doorkeeper. I am a poet and a historian."

"We do not need you. We already have a poet and historian, En mac Ethamain."

He said, "Question me. I am a sorcerer."

"We do not need you. We have sorcerers already. Our druids and our people of power are numerous."

He said, "Question me. I am a physician."

"We do not need you. We have Dian Ceacht as a physician."

He said, "Question me. I am a cupbearer."

"We do not need you. We have cupbearers already: Delt and Drucht and Daithe; Tae and Talom and Trog; Gle and Glan and Glesse."

He said, "Question me. I am a good brazier."

"We do not need you. We have a brazier already,
Credne Cerd."[8]

This formal set of questions and answers is repeated in various forms throughout the legend. It seems obvious that this was no ordinary conversation, but rather a clearly defined, ritualistic communication. Note that Lugh starts every statement with the command, "Question me," but the doorkeeper never does. The doorkeeper always starts his reply with a negative statement, "We do not need you." This verbal exchange was as much a right of passage to Tara as were the physical skills of Lugh. The answers the doorkeeper gives, on the surface, are a bit odd. Why does he say they have only one champion and one warrior, yet later in the legend it becomes clear that there were many warriors at Tara? Why are nine cupbearers mentioned by name, yet the powerful and important druids and sorcerers are not named at all? Could this suggest magical content with greater implications than a simple conversation between a doorkeeper and Lugh?

In a passage from the twelfth-century *Book of Leinster*, there is a similar exchange between two sages, Feircheirdne (fer-chayr-nay) and Neidhe (nee-thay), which takes place when Feircheirdne challenges the newcomer's right to sit in the chair of the poet.

"A question, wise lad, whence have you come?"

Neidhe answered,

"Not hard: from the heel of a sage,

From a confluence of wisdom,

From perfection of goodness,

---

[8] E. A. Gray, trans., *Cath Maige Tuired* (Dublin: Irish Texts Society, 1983).

18

From the brightness of the sunrise,

From the nine hazels of poetic art,

From splendid circuits, in a land

Where truth is measured by excellence,

Where there is no falsehood,

Where there are many colors,

Where poets are refreshed.

And thou, O my master, whence have you come?"

Feircheirdne answered,

"Not hard: down the columns of age,

Along the streams of Gaileoin,

From the fairymound of Neachtan's wife,

From the land of the sun,

From the dwelling of the moon,

Along Mac ind Oc's navel string.

A question, O wise lad, what is thy name?"

Neidhe answered,

"Not hard: very small, very great, very bright, very hard,

Angriness of fire,

Fire of speech,

Noise of knowledge,

Well of wisdom,

Sword of song,

I sing straight from the heart of the fire.

And you, O aged one, what is your name?"

Feircheirdne answered,

"Not hard: questioner, declarer, champion of song,

Inquiry of science,

Weft of art,

Casket of poetry,

Abundance from the sea of knowledge.

A question, O youthful instructor, what art
do you practice?"

Neidhe answered,

"Not hard: reddening of countenance,

Flesh-piercing satire,

Promoting bashfulness,

Disposing of shamelessness,

Fostering poetry,

Searching for fame,

Wooing science,

Art for every mouth,

Diffusing knowledge,

Stripping speech,

In a little room

Making poems like a sage's cattle,

A stream of science,

Abundant teaching,

Polished tales, the delight of kings.

And you, O my elder, what art do you practice?"

Feircheirdne answered,

"Not hard: hunting for the treasure of knowledge,

Establishing peace,

Arranging words in ranks,

Celebrating art,

Sharing a pallet with a king,

Drinking the Boyne,

Making briarmon smetrach,

The shield of Aithirne,

A tribulation to all men,

A share of wisdom from the stream of science,

Fury of inspiration,

Structure of mind,

Art of small poems,

Clear arrangement of words,

Warrior tales,

Walking the great road,

Like a pearl in its setting,

Giving strength to science through the poetic art.

A question, O youthful instructor, what are your tasks?"

Neidhe answered,

"Not hard: to go to the plain of age,

To the mountain of youth,

To the hunting of age,

To follow a king,

Into an abode of clay,

Between candle and fire,

Between battle and horrors,

Among the people of the Fomhoire,

Among streams of knowledge.

And you, O sage, what are your tasks?"

Feircheirdne answered,

"Not hard: to go into the mountain of rank,

The communion of sciences,

The lands of knowledgeable men,

Into the breast of poetic vision,

The estuary of bountiful wisdom,

To the fair of the Great Boar,

To find respect among men,

To go into death's hills,

Where I may find a great honor.

A question, O knowledgeable lad, by what path
have you come?"

Neidhe answered,

"Not hard: on the white plain of knowledge,

On a king's beard,

On a wood of age,

On the back of a ploughing ox,

On the light of a summer's moon,

On rich mast and food,

On the corn and milk of a goddess,

On thin corn,

On a narrow ford,

On my own strong thighs.

And you, O sage, by what path have you come?"

Feircheirdne answered,

"Not hard: on Lugh's horserod,

On the breasts of soft women,

On a line of wood,

On the head of a spear,

On a gown of silver,

On a chariot without a wheelrim,

On a wheelrim without a chariot,

On the threefold ignorance of Mac ind Oc.

And you, O knowledgeable lad, whose son are you?"

Neidhe answered,

"Not hard: I am the son of poetry,

Poetry son of scrutiny,

Scrutiny son of meditation,

Meditation son of lore,

Lore son of enquiry,

Enquiry son of investigation,

Investigation son of great knowledge,

Great knowledge son of great sense,

Great sense son of understanding,

Understanding son of wisdom,

Wisdom son of the triple gods of poetry."[9]

The full passage goes on, but this extract shows again the very rigid and ritualistic manner of speech—this time between poets. This structure was as much a part of the information being exchanged as were the answers themselves. Note also that the replies start with a negative statement, "Not hard," which was the style used by Lugh at Tara's gates, and also in the earlier quotation from the *Book of Ballymote* regarding the numbers connected with Ogham.[10]

---

[9] Dr. W. Stokes, trans., *Book of Leinster*, (Dublin: Dublin Institute for Advanced Studies, 1973).

[10] A spoken version of the above exchange, known as "The Dialogue of the Two Sages," can be found on Robin Williamson's cassette *Five Bardic Mysteries*, where it can be heard as it was originally meant to be. See the Discography.

In a legend from the Ulster Cycle[11] known as *Tochmarc Emire*, the "Wooing of Eimhear," the hero Cuchulain has a similar encounter with the Lady Eimhear, whom he has come to woo.

> Then Eimhear lifted up her lovely face and said to him, "Where are you come from?" He replied in riddles so that her companions would not understand what was exchanged between them and he said, "Not hard to answer. From Intide Emna."
>
> Eimhear asked of him, "Where did you sleep?" and he replied, "Not hard to answer. In the house belonging to the man that tends the cattle of the plain of Tethra."
>
> "What did you eat there?" she asked. "Not hard to answer. The ruin of a chariot."
>
> She asked, "Which way did you come here?" and he said, "Not hard to answer. Between the Two Mountains of the Wood; from the cover of the sea; over the Great Secret of the Tuatha De Danann; the Foam of the Horses of Eamhain; over the Mor-Rioghain's Garden and the Great Sow's back; over the Valley of the Great Dam; between the God and his Druid; over the Marrow of the Woman between the Boar and his Dam; over the Washing Place of Dea's Horses; between the King of Ana and his Servant; to Muincille of the Four Corners of the World; over Great Wrong-Doing and the Remnants of the Great Feast; between the Great Vat and the Little Vat to the Gardens of Lugh, to the daughters of Tethra."

---

[11] The Ulster Cycle is a collective term for a vast body of legends centering on the adventures of King Conchobhar and his Knights of the Red Branch. Their greatest hero was the Ulster warrior Cuchulain.

"What account of yourself do you have?" asked Eimhear. "Not hard to answer," he said, "I am the nephew of a man that disappears in another in the wood of Badhbh."

"What account can you give to me?" asked Cuchulain. "Not hard to answer," replied Eimhear, "I am Tara upon the hill; a watcher but see no one; an eel in water; a rush out of reach. The daughter of a king is a flame of hospitality and a road that is barred. I have following champions to keep me from hostage takers."

"Who are these champions?" asked Cuchulain. "Not hard to answer, Luath and Lath Goible mac Tethra; Triath and Trescath; Brion and Balur; Bas mac Omnach; Condla and Cond son of Forgall. Every one of them has the strength of a hundred and the feats of nine. Forgall himself is stronger than any, more learned than the druids, more quick of mind than the poets."

"What is your strength?" Eimhear asked Cuchulain. He replied, "Not hard to answer. When I am at my weakest I defend twenty, a third of my strength is enough to defend thirty but at my full strength I fight forty and protect a hundred men."[12]

This was no ordinary conversation between two lovers. Indeed, in the first paragraph, it is stated that they chose this form of speech so that the girls with Eimhear would not understand what they were really saying to each other. Only a person such as a druid, bard, magician, or poet, versed in Ogham or familiar with the use of what were known as "kennings"—poetic allusions to people and things couched in highly symbolic terms—would have been able to interpret this conversation. To anyone without this special knowledge it would sound like a lot of garbled nonsense.

---

[12] Eleanor Hull, trans., *Cuchulain: Hound of Ulster* (London, 1911).

The latest reference in the manuscripts to Ogham as a type of speech comes from an entry in the *Annals of Clonmacnoise* for the year 1328:

> Morish O'Gibelan, master of art, one exceedingly well learned in the new and old ways, civil and cannon, a cunning and skillful philosopher, an excellent poet in Irish, an eloquent and exact speaker of the speech which in Irish is called Ogham, and one that was well seen in many other good sciences.[13]

Finally, we can say the original Ogham, which has always been linked to the champion Oghma, turns out to be a style of address used as a means of recognition or testing between heroes, champions, bards, and druids. Its name was only later given to the written alphabet used on standing stones, but this was quite some time after its original spoken use had lapsed. If we consider the importance of the spoken word in magical Workings, it becomes clear that we must consider Ogham in its true form—as a ritualistic manner of speech—and familiarize ourselves with its grammar and structure.

Of course, the question arises: If Ogham is a form of speech, to whom should we be speaking? I would contend that we should be talking to the trees and to our own Inner or Higher Self. Deep communication and dialogue with the trees and our true Self allows us to benefit from the instruction they can give us. This is a non-verbal dialogue, however, which takes place on the mental and spiritual levels, as you will discover in the Practical Work to come.

---

[13] *Annals of Clonmacnoise.* (Dublin: Dublin Institute for Advanced Studies, 1953).

CHAPTER TWO

THE VALIDITY OF THE TREE CALENDAR

Lists of correspondences between Ogham characters and everything imaginable seem to be obligatory in modern books about Celtic magic. These lists are drawn from a variety of sources, some accepted, some questionable, and have become very popular with Celtic revivalist groups and practitioners of old Pagan religions. Many of these "magical tables" of correspondences are no more than examples of Oghams like those in Chapter One. As we know, these were never intended to be magical source lists, but rather to provide grammatical understanding.

One prevalent Ogham association concerns the calendar and the marking of time. In this system, dates correspond to Tree Ogham characters, and by extension, to their corresponding trees. So popular has this notion become, that many books refer to it as the "Celtic tree calendar." This is not, however, derived from ancient Celtic practice and belief, nor is it mentioned in the manuscripts dealing with Ogham.

The Celtic tree calendar notion seems to have stemmed from a book called *The White Goddess*, by Robert Graves, which was first published in 1947.[1] In this work, Mr. Graves examines the Ogham characters, and in particular, the Tree Ogham. In my opinion, he fails to stress sufficiently that the connection between trees and the Ogham script is only one such connection, but not the only one. There are over a hundred different Oghams in the books of Ballymote, Lecan, and Leinster; and according to these sources, poets had to learn at least one hundred and fifty different Oghams, all of which were used to illustrate grammatical laws and instructions, not the passing of time.

For individuals who have worked out Oghmic correspondences for themselves, and not simply copied them from books, there may be a validity and practical magical use, but it should be understood that these are not authentic, ancient Celtic associations. Some writers may be sincere in their belief that they have somehow "cracked the secret of Ogham" as a magical system, but that must assume that there was a secret to crack. Considering that not even a hint of such a calendrical system has been suggested by any eminent Celtic scholar for the hundreds of years prior to 1947, how likely does this seem?

If we take a look at what we do know about the Celtic view of time, it soon becomes clear that trees and months simply do not enter into it. To the early Celts time simply *was*. Everything was here and now. The concepts of past and future rarely occur in the old writings. The legends make almost no references to past or future events, the narrative being almost entirely in the present tense. The later Celts, especially the Christian Celts, adopted a form

---

[1] Robert Graves, *The White Goddess* (London: Rider, 1947).

of marking time, but even this did not involve trees or any other form of Ogham.

The main time span by which the pre-Christian Celts dated events was known as the Great Year. This was a span of approximately nineteen solar years, and is best explained as the full cycle of the sun, moon, and earth. The sun will always rise and set at the same point on the horizon, on the same date each year, although it will be in a slightly different position on each consecutive day throughout the year. In other words, where the sun rose this morning will be exactly the same place it will rise one year from now, but it will not be the same place tomorrow. (The sun shines down the entrance passage to the great megalithic burial chamber known as Newgrange, in the Boyne Valley, every year on the day of the Winter Solstice, but at no other time.) The moon, however, takes roughly nineteen years to return to the same rising and setting position on the horizon. A Great Year is, therefore, the time it takes the sun and moon to go through their complete cycles and coincide again at the same rising and setting positions.

You can start a Great Year cycle any day you like, and it will always be nineteen years until the sun and moon coincide again. The nineteen-year cycles are determined by a physical location on the surface of the earth, and not by a fixed day or date. Newgrange may have been used to determine the passing of the Great Year, but there is no evidence to that effect (other than its obvious physical function). Other important sites such as Tara, Uisneach, or Eamhain Macha could have been used just as effectively. We no longer know when the Great Year cycles that the druids may have used on a consecutive basis started and finished, nor can we be sure just what significance the Great Year had in their magical workings, or how or if it was celebrated.

Another dating system mentioned in several modern books on the druids is a five-year cycle of rituals and observances. This system is based on the Coligny Calendar, a large, bronze tablet found in France in 1897. Although only fragments remain, there is enough to indicate that it once formed the basis for some kind of calendar. It has months inscribed upon it spanning a five-year period, and beside each name is a little hole, as if pegs or some other marking device were to be inserted into them.

The truth is that we do not know whether the Coligny Calendar was druidic at all. Recent research indicates that it may well be a later Roman attempt to copy a Gaulish—not necessarily druidic—system; but it may never have served any ritualistic or magical function.

To further complicate matters, the earliest Christian scribes in Ireland used an eighty-four year cycle to place events in time. This has lead to difficulty when trying to determine exact dates from the ancient annals, as it is often not clear whether the writer was using the eighty-four year cycle, or our hundred-year cycle, or if he, himself, was confusing dates from one cycle as being from the other. Imagine today if a date is given without its relevant century (e.g., "It happened in '68." What '68? 1968? 1868? 1368?). Consider the greater problem of dating events when some annals use dates such as '45 or '32, and we do not even know upon which cycle they are based.

We don't even know why a cycle of eighty-four years should have been used in the first place. The only people likely to have been concerned with dating methods, keeping annals, and recording historical data were the druids, so this eighty-four year cycle may be a relic of ancient druidic practice. This still does not tell us when or how it was used. It has been suggested that eighty-four may have been chosen because this is the number of days of the week multiplied by the number of months of the year. This still does not explain why this was important.

You can see how little we know of druidic or Celtic dating systems. What we can say is that none of the known systems is based on the counting of months, and none of them is connected with trees. However, magic and symbolism are evolving things. It is acceptable for individuals or groups to devise their own symbol systems based on the Ogham scripts; there is nothing wrong with creating a modern interpretation of an ancient system. For my part, I have concentrated on the useful and practical Tree Ogham, rather than the less practical and relatively useless tree calendar. I find that an understanding of the natural trees of the forest helps to explain much about the Irish legends. We will explore this in Part Three; but first we will look at the individual trees that make up the Tree Ogham, and how to know them and learn from them.

CHAPTER THREE

THE DEVELOPMENT OF THE TREE OGHAM

The double list of letters, names, and trees taken from the *Book of Ballymote* appears in many manuscript sources (see the Bibliography), where they are discussed separately from the Ogham script itself (see Table One, p. 36). Although the initial letters of each tree, and their order, are the same as the letters given for the Ogham notches, these lists are intended to be regarded separately from the basic Ogham script.

These two almost identical lists have provided the basis for many references to Tree Ogham, both ancient and modern works. The *Book of Ballymote* offers two lists because of slight grammatical differences in the use of the letters. We no longer know why these differences are important, and have seen no consistent use of Ogham which demonstrates these differences. If you study other sources, you

TABLE ONE

The Tree Alphabets As Given in the Book of Ballymote[1]

LETTER	NAME	TREE	LETTER	NAME	TREE
B	Beithe	Birch	B	Beith	Birch
L	Luis	Rowan	L	Luis	Rowan
F	Fearn	Alder	F	Fearn	Alder
S	Sail	Willow	S	Sail	Willow
N	Nion	Ash	N	Nion	Ash
H	Huath	Hawthorn	H	Huath	Hawthorn
D	Duir	Oak	D	Duir	Oak
T	Tinne	Holly	T	Tinne	
C	Coll	Hazel	C	Coll	Hazel
Q	Queirt	Apple	Q	Queirt	Apple
M	Muin	Vine	M	Muin	Vine
G	Gort	Ivy	G	Gort	Ivy
nG	nGetal	Broom	nG	nGetal	Reed
St	Sraibh	Blackthorn	P	Pethboc	
R	Ruis	Elder	St	Straiph	Sloe
A	Ailm	Fir	R	Ruis	Elder
O	Onn	Furze	A	Ailm	Fir
U	Ur	Heather	O	Onn	Furze
E	Edhadh	Aspen	U	Ur	Heather
I	Ido	Yew	E	Eadhadh	Aspen
EA	Ebhadh	Aspen	I	Idhadh	Yew
OI	Oir	Ivy	EA	Eabhadh	Aspen
UI	Uilleand	Honeysuckle	OI	Oir	Ivy
IO	Iphin	Gooseberry	UI	Uilleann	Woodbine
			IO	Ifin	Gooseberry
			AE	Amhancholl	

---

[1] Unless otherwise stated, all quotations are from *The Scholar's Primer*, translated by George Calder (Edinburgh: Long, 1917).

will find that some writers have shortened the lists, some have changed letter-to-tree associations, and some have added other correspondences that do not appear in the originals.

According to tradition, this alphabet, and the order of its letters, was composed by one Fenius Farsaidh, with the help of Goidel mac Etheoir and Iar mac Nema. The legend tells us that Fenius was in the Holy Land at the time of the construction of the Tower of Babel. The Bible states that, at this time, there was a single, common language spoken by all the peoples of the earth. When this common language was changed, corrupted, and distorted by God as His punishment for the attempts of the people to reach Him by building the tower, Fenius sent his seventy-two scholars throughout the world to study and learn all of these new languages. After ten years, the scholars returned to the tower, and Fenius selected the best from all of the world's languages and created *in Berla tobaide*, the "selected language." The common name given to this newly invented language was *Goidelic*, named after Goidel mac Etheoir. This was the forerunner to Gaelic. By way of thanks to his hardest working scholars, Fenius named the letters of this new language after them. This list became known by its first two letters, *Bobel Loth*, which also means the "Destruction of Babel." The list of letters as given in *Auraicept Na nEces (The Scholar's Primer)* is shown in Table Two (p. 38). The same passage explains the addition of the *forfeda*, the supplementary characters.

> What was best accordingly of every language and what was widest and finest was selected for Gaelic; and for every sound for which no characters were found in all other alphabets, characters were by them found for these in the Beithe Luis Nion of the Ogham:

EA OI UI IO AE

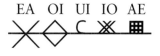

TABLE TWO

The Bobel Loth Alphabet

LETTER	TEACHER'S NAME
B	Bobel
L	Loth
F	Foronn
S	Saliath
N	Nabgadon
H	Hiruath
D	Davith
T	Talemon
C	Cai
Q	Qualep
M	Mareth
G	Gath
nG	nGoimer
Sd	Stru
R	Ruben
A	Achab
O	Ose
U	Uriath
E	Etrocuis
I	Iachim

Whether or not the Bobel Loth alphabet ever had a magical function we do not know, but it is doubtful because the above quotation is the only reference to it in all the manuscripts dealing with Ogham. It is interesting to note, however, that the invention of this whole script and language was attributed to one man. Scholars in this complex field are of a similar opinion regarding the origins of Ogham.

The name given to the Tree Ogham, *Beithe Luis Nion,* is inconsistent with the theory that the name, like our "ABCs," was derived from the original first three letters of the alphabet. The first three letters we use today are *Beithe, Luis, Fearn.* This has caused speculation as to whether we have a corrupted version of the order of the letters, or if the name itself has been changed. It could be that the name *Beithe Luis Nion* is correct, the order of the letters is correct, and the name actually stands for something else. Some have suggested that the letters derive from the name of the Celtic god, BeLiNos. We can also find some words in Irish and Scottish Gaelic containing these three consonants, which are, perhaps, more relevant to the Tree Ogham and its applications.

For example, there is the word *BaLlaN,* which means a natural cup-like hole in a stone, and possibly ring stones or even Ogham stones. The word *BeaLaN* means "little mouth" or "mouthful," which again suggests Ogham as an oral tradition. There is a word in Gaelic that has no direct, one-word equivalent in English, *BLiNn,* which means a dead man's spittle. This may be connected with the curious association given to Sail/Willow, as we shall see in Chapter Eight. Two important characters from Arthurian tradition, which has its ancient roots in Celtic mythology, are *BaLiN* and *BaLaN,* who also bear these three important consonants in their names. It may be that the title, *Beithe Luis Nion,* is a cryptic reference to the magical use of the Tree Ogham rather than a corrupted form of the first three letters. There is also an Old Irish word, *BiLe* (plural *BiLeN*), meaning "sacred tree," which clearly connects with Tree Ogham.

Anyone familiar with modern Scottish or Irish Gaelic will note that there are several letters in the *Beithe Luis Nion* that do not occur in the modern Gaelic alphabet. These additional letters, and combinations of letters, probably came from Latin and the Roman alphabet. Comments in the manuscripts imply that the monks of the day were familiar with written Gaelic as well as Latin, which may have resulted in some grammatical changes. While these are not magical concerns, an understanding of these changes has implications for our use of the Tree Ogham as a magical system. The *Auraicept* says:

> H first. It increases B until it acquires the force of P, B for aspiration is put for P, so that H increases it, for P is the aspiration of the Gael. Full power is in them both vowels and consonants with the exception of H.

H does not exist in the Gaelic language as a letter in its own right. You will find it written in Gaelic text, but only as an indication that the letter succeeding or preceding it will change in sound. For example, you will sometimes find Gaelic words where the letters B and M are followed by the letter H, which has the effect of changing the sound of the letter B or M to a V sound, another letter which does not exist in the Gaelic alphabet. The letter H "increases" the strength of the B. In short, the letter H is not a letter, but more of an accent affecting other letters. If H is neither vowel nor consonant, it must be something else. This implies that, within the Tree Ogham, it must have some significance different from the other letters and trees. We shall consider this important point fully in Chapter Ten.

The letter P did not originally appear in written Gaelic either, although the P sound existed in the spoken language. This sound was represented by a B when written. This is still the case today, where a B is often pronounced as a P, such as in the Scottish-Gaelic name for Scotland, *Alba* (al-ah-pah).

The *Auraicept* goes on to comment on the other non-Gaelic combinations of letters in the Tree Ogham:

> Three component letters of the Ogham exist, Qu, nG and Sr.
>
> Where C stands before U it is Queirt that is to be written;
>
> where N stands before G it is nGetal that is to be written;
>
> where S stands before D it is Straiph that is to be written.

Once again this indicates that these letter groupings are not letters in their own right, but combinations to be used only in certain circumstances. Like the letter H, if they were removed from the Tree Ogham, we would be left with the letters and trees that actually make up the basis of the modern Gaelic alphabet.

The last group of letters, which are not relevant to the Gaelic language and the construction of proper Gaelic words, are the double vowels—the *forfeda*—shown at the end of the two lists in Table One. These five double-vowel groups were invented by Fenius solely because no other letters could be found to symbolize these specific sounds in Gaelic. It is fair to assume that these *artificial* groupings cannot be considered part of the *Beithe Luis Nion* proper, which is composed of the "*natural* trees of the forest."

Finally, it should be noted that the letters D and T were originally more or less interchangeable. They are listed one after the other in both the *Beithe Luis Nion* and the *Bobel Loth*. Also note that, in one of the letter-to-tree lists given in Table One, T is allocated a tree, the holly, yet in the other it is not. It has been argued that the holly referred to here is actually the holly-oak, and this strengthens the connection between D and T, as the letter D has been allocated the oak proper. In *Dinneen's Irish Dictionary*[2] it says that T often takes the place of D before vowels, and that D eclipses

---

[2] *Dinneen's Irish Dictionary* (Dublin: Irish Texts Society, 1927).

T. In de Bhaldraithe's 1978 edition of the *Irish-English Dictionary*,[3] this point is made as well. In *Maclennan's Scottish Gaelic Dictionary*[4] it is noted that T is used for "d" or "do" (thy) when placed before a word beginning with a vowel or aspiration. This aspect of the T being a lesser form of D (the oak, a symbol for the High King) is reflected in ancient Irish social practice, where the king had a second, or double, who was called a *Tainaiste*. The king's *Tainaiste* was almost as important as the king and, in some circumstances, actually took the place of the king. This word is still used today in the Irish parliamentary system to refer to the deputy Prime Minister. The word *Tainaiste* has its roots in the word *Tinne*, as does the English word tannin, the sap of the oak. The oak, letter D, has been called the "king of the trees," and the holly, letter T, is its *Tainaiste*, or substitute.

The letter called *Pethboc*, in the right hand list in Table One, is actually a corruption of *Beithe Beag*, which means "little birch." It also means "soft B." A soft B is the letter P, which did not exist in Old Irish. Our basic Tree Ogham is now as shown in Table Three (p. 43). The letters and trees we have eliminated from the original list are still useful, and do play a part, but only in conjunction with one or more of the basic trees of the alphabet. This is the way they function on the magical side, too, one symbolizing the other.

As we proceed, it will be necessary to refer back and forth between the Tree Ogham and the grammatical instructions for the written Ogham. Perhaps the easiest way to cope with this is to keep in mind that the "spoken" language of the trees is in reality an inner, mental, abstract process. To engage this process, however, it is necessary to know how it developed. Fortunately, the *Book of Ballymote*, as quoted in the *Auraicept*, gives us quite a bit of information on the nature of trees and how they got their Ogham names.

---

[3] de Bhaldraithe, *Irish-English Dictionary* (1978).
[4] Malcolm Maclennan, *Scottish Gaelic Dictionary* (Acair: Edinburgh, 1925), 329.

The Basic Tree Ogham Alphabet

LETTER	NAME	TREE
B	Beithe	Birch
L	Luis	Rowan
F	Fearn	Alder
S	Sail	Willow
N	Nion	Ash
H	Huath	Hawthorn
D	Duir	Oak
T	Tinne	Holly
C	Coll	Hazel
Q	Queirt	Apple
M	Muin	Vine
G	Gort	Ivy
nG	nGetal	Broom
St	Straiph	Blackthorn
R	Ruis	Elder
A	Ailm	Fir
O	Onn	Furze
U	Ur	Heather
E	Eadhadh	Aspen
I	Idhadh	Yew

Now *Beithe* has been named from the Birch owing to its resemblance to the trunk of that tree. Of withered trunk, fair-haired the Birch.

Luis is named from Mountain Ash as it is the old Gaelic name for the tree. Delight of eye is Mountain Ash owing to the beauty of its berries.

Fearn, Alder, the van of the warrior bands for thereof are the shields.

Sail, Willow, the color of a lifeless one, owing to the resemblance of its color to a dead person.

Nion, Ash, a check on peace is Nion for of it are made the spear-shafts by which the peace is broken.

Huath is Whitethorn, a meet of hounds is Whitethorn, it is formidable owing to its thorns.

Duir, Oak, higher than bushes is an Oak.

Tinne, Holly, a third of a wheel is Holly, because Holly is one of the three timbers of the chariot wheel.

Coll, fair wood that is Hazel everyone is eating of its nuts.

Queirt, Apple, shelter of a wild hind is an Apple tree.

Muin is a Vine tree highest of beauty is Muin because it grows aloft.

Gort that is Ivy, Greener than Pastures is Ivy.

nGetal, Broom or Fern, a physician's strength is Broom.

Straiph that is Blackthorn, the hedge of a stream is Sraibh.

Ruis is Elder, the redness of shame.

Ailm, a Fir tree, a Pine tree.

Onn that is Furze.

Ur that is Heath.

Edhadh (*Ed Uath*: "horrible grief") Test tree or Aspen.

Ido, Yew.

This listing gives us a hint of each tree's qualities and functions, yet the above comments are superficial and intended to provide only a very basic level of understanding for those coming new to the subject. We want to know something deeper; something which will help us to gain insight into the Otherworld and the magical meanings and uses of trees. The compilers of these important source works give three lists of names and descriptions for each tree, which tell us a great deal more about them. The first of these is known as the Word Ogham of Morainn mac Moin. It was reputedly composed by Morainn, who was a great judge well-known for his good decisions and scrupulously fair dealings in all cases brought before him.

B equals *FEOCHAS FOLTCHAIN*, faded trunk and fair hair.

L equals *LI SULA*, delight of eye.

F equals *AIREINECH FIANN*, shield of warrior bands.

S equals *LI AMBI*, hue of the lifeless.

N equals *COSTUD SIDE*, checking of peace.

H equals *CONDAL CON*, pack of wolves (or hounds).

D equals *ARDDAM DOSSA*, highest of bushes and *TRIAN* a third.

T equals *TRIAN ROITH*, third of a wheel.

C equals *CAINIU FEDAIB*, fairest of trees.

Q equals *CLITHCHAR BOSCILL*, shelter of a hind, *BOSCELL* equals lunatic, *BAS CEALL* equals death sense, the time when a lunatic's senses come back to him. Therefore *CLITHCHAR mBAISCAILL* means shelter of lunatics.

M equals *ARDAM MAISI*, highest of beauty, *TRESIM FEDMA*, strongest of effort, *MUIN* equals back of man or ox for it is they in existence that are strongest as regards effort.

G equals *GLAISEM GELTA*, greenest of pastures, *MILLSIU FERAIB*, sweeter than grasses, due to associations with corn fields.

nG equals *LUTH LEIGHE*, a physician's strength, *CATH* equals panacea. *GETAL* equals Broom.

St equals *AIRE SRABHA*, careful effort, *TRESIM RUAMNA*, strongest of red. *STRAIPH* equals sloe which gives strong red dye on metal.

R equals *TINNEM RUICE*, intensest of blushes, it is reddening that grows on a man's face through the juice of the herb being rubbed on it.

A equals *ARDAM IACHTADHA*, loudest of groanings, that is, wondering. *AILM* or A for that is what a man says while groaning in disease or wonder.

O equals *CONGNAID ECH*, helper of horses. *ONNAID* equals wheels of a chariot. *ALITER COMGUINIDECH*, equally wounding. Whin.

U equals *GRUIDEM DAL*, terrible tribe, *UARAIB ADBAIB*, in cold dwellings. *UIR* equals mould of the earth. *UR* equals Heath.

E equals *AERCNAID FER NO FID*, distinguished man or wood.

I equals *SINEM FEDHA*, oldest of woods. *IBUR* equals service tree, Yew.

Don't be put off by the complicated spellings, and by the way the spellings change in mid-sentence. The Old or Middle Irish names are not the point. The point is what these names mean and how they can be used in a practical way.

The second list is attributed to the great Ulster hero, Cuchulain, who we know was well-acquainted with Ogham. The ".i." is an Irish abbreviation for "that is" or, as it would be shown in English, "i.e."

B equals *MAISI MALACH .i. CRECCAD*, browed beauty, worthy of pursuit.

L equals *LUTH CETHRA .i. LEAM*, strength of cattle, the elm.

F equals *DIN CRIDE .i. SCIATH*, protection of the heart, a shield.

S equals *TOSACH MELA .i. SAIL*, beginning of loss, willow.

N equals *BAG MAISI .i. GARMAN*, flight (or boast) of beauty, a weaver's beam.

H equals *ANNSAM AIDHCHE .i. HUATH*, difficult night, hawthorn.

D equals *SLECHTAIN SAIRE .i. NIAMA SAIRTE*, kneeling work, bright and shining work.

T equals *TRIAN N-AIRM .i. TINNE IAIRN*, a third of weapons, an iron bar.

C equals *MILLSEM FEDHO .i. CNO*, sweetest of woods, a nut.

Q equals *DIGHU FETHAIL .i. CUMDAIGH*, excellent emblem, protection.

M equals *CONAIR GOTHA .i. TRE MUIN*, pack of wolves with spears, three vines.

G equals *SASADH ILE .i. ARBHAR*, pleasing oil, corn.

nG equals *TOSACH N-ECHTO .i. ICCE*, beginning of heroic deeds, healing.

St equals *SAIGID NEL .i. A DDE SUAS*, an arrow's mist, smoke drifting up from the fire.

R equals *BRUTH FERGGA .i. IMDERGADH*, arduous anger, punishment.

A equals *TOSACH GARMA .i. A*, beginning of the weavers' beams, ahh.

O equals *LUTH FIANN .i. FRAECH*, strength of warriors, fierceness.

U equals *FORBHAID AMBI .i. UIR*, completion of lifelessness, the grave.

E equals *BRATHAIR BETHI .i. E*, kinsman to the birch, aspen.

I equals *LUTH (NO LITH) LOBAIR .i. AES*, strength (or color) of a sick man, people or an age.

A third list of trees and meanings is attributed to the god Aonghus.

B equals *GLAISEM CNIS*, most silver of skin.

L equals *CARAE CEATHRA*, friend of cattle.

F equals *COIMET LACHTA*, guarding of milk (or milk container).

S equals *LUTH BEACH*, strength of bees.

N equals *BAG BAN*, the flight (or perhaps boast) of women.

H equals *BANAD GNUISI*, whitening of face.

D equals *GRES SAIR*, craft work (or perhaps carpenter's work).

T equals *SMIUR GUAILE*, fires of coal.

C equals *CARA BLOISC*, friend of cracking.

Q equals *BRIG ANDUINE*, force of a man.

M equals *MARUSC N-AIRLIG*, the condition of slaughter.

G equals *MED NERCC*, size of a warrior.

nG equals *EITIUD MIDACH*, robe of physicians.

St equals *MORAD RUN*, increasing of secrets.

R equals *ROMNAD DRECH*, redness of faces.

A equals *TOSACH FREGRA*, beginning of answers.

O equals *FOILLEM SAIRE*, gentlest of work.

U equals *SILAD CLAND*, growing of plants.

E equals *COMMAIN CARAT*, additional name for a friend.

I equals *CAINED SEN NO AILEAM AIS*, abuse for an ancestor or pleasing consent.

These three lists follow similar patterns and provide similar descriptions of tree letters; however, they are not corrupted forms of one another, nor of some common source, but are different interpretations of a common Ogham. I refer to these three interpretations as the "Word Oghams" throughout the rest of this book.

Morainn's Word Ogham is very straightforward, and may well have been a Word Ogham for beginners. We know from legends that Morainn was a great poet and very skilled in the use of words. It is said he was born with a caul on his head, which was removed by immersing him in the sea, where the ninth wave washed it off. This immersion in the sea is clearly an initiatory rite, and the important ninth wave, which is always associated with poetic inspiration, indicates that Morainn was destined to be important. His story continues with the caul becoming a collar which he placed around the neck of people being questioned by him. If they told a lie it would shrink and strangle them, if they told the truth it would remain as it was and do them no harm. Any magical system devised by such a powerful character is worthy of study.

The Word Ogham of Cuchulain contains many expressions and allusions intended to be used by the warrior caste to which he belonged. Aonghus's Word Ogham is much more abstract and confusing than the others, which is to be expected of a deity well known for his riddles and pranks. These three lists are connected in that they could represent the Three Levels of Being. Morainn, a purely physical being of this world, could represent the physical level; Cuchulain may represent the mental level in that, although he is human, he has the ability to move about in the Otherworld and perform superhuman feats; and Aonghus, being a god, could represent the spiritual level. This may not have been the intention of the compilers of the source works, but it nonetheless fits the world view of existence on three levels. (See my book *Glamoury: Magic of the Celtic Green World* for a full discussion of the three levels.)

We will use these Word Oghams to decipher the mysterious secrets of the Tree Ogham and for practical, magical uses. We will concentrate on the Word Ogham of Morainn, as this is the most straightforward and easiest to interpret. The other two Word Oghams are provided to help as you study the principles and techniques in the following chapters, developing your own interpretations and practical uses.

PART
TWO

CHAPTER FOUR

THE THREE LEVELS OF THE TREES

There is no point in expressing an interest in the magical aspect of Ogham and trees without first knowing the physical properties of the trees themselves. The overemphasis on the magical aspects of trees has not been a good thing. It has detracted from their other important properties, not least being their function as the creators and filters of the atmosphere of the planet, something which is truly magical and upon which every other life form on Earth depends.

In the following chapters, we shall examine each tree in detail on each of its three levels. Next, we will look at how the individual properties of trees and their attributions change when they interact with each other. This is the key to the study of the Tree Ogham. As you progress, you will build a body of practical magical knowledge and skill that you should be able to use on all of your levels of existence, especially the spiritual. This emphasis on the spiritual aspect is one of the main differences between this and other popular forms of magic.

What you will be doing is learning to read and write in another language by first becoming familiar with the individual letters of the alphabet, and then by combining them to see what acceptable results you can obtain. With practice, you should be able to read the trees just as you would the words on this page. You will find that some trees (letters) appear together more frequently than others, while some associations will never be found. This is just like the rules governing the use of letters in any written language. A deep understanding of this tree grammar is an integral part of successful tree magic.

Most people with sufficient practice and guidance can develop a basic knowledge of the properties and characteristics of each tree on its three levels. A few will go on to group these trees in ways that make sense; however, these skills are not the same as actually speaking the language of the trees. For instance, you could attempt to learn Greek by memorizing the Greek alphabet and learning Greek spelling and grammar, but these would not teach you the myriad of nuances, inflections, and idioms that distinguish the fluent speaker. So it is with the trees. I can teach you to recognize the trees and what they mean, and I can give you a grounding in tree combinations and tree grammar, but it will be up to you to learn to speak the language of the trees fluently. You can do this by taking the time and making the effort to find each tree in its natural habitat, and by coming into close communion with it and the Green World. You must know the trees: their bark, leaves, and shapes, and the life that exists on and around them. Celtic tradition teaches total involvement in the things of this world, and a very solid and deep spiritual link with the land.

We will start with an examination of each tree. Then we will consider examples of messages and subtle magical instruction provided by the trees in combination. First, however, we will discuss how you can begin your practical studies as you learn about the trees.

Introduction to the Practical Work

The practice of tree magic is a very personal thing, perhaps more so than any other form of magic. A deep, personal relationship with each tree must be established before any progress can be made. What follows are basic guidelines for Practical Work. You may find yourself developing your own system, and if so, do it; always follow your intuition in such matters. Initially, however, I would suggest you work your way through this set of tried and tested exercises.

If at all possible, perform the Practical Work outdoors and close to the tree you are studying. If outdoor Working is not possible, or if a certain species of tree is not available in your area, then indoor Working with a branch, twig, leaf, or fruit of the tree can be substituted. If you are Working outdoors, you should perform these exercises in all weather conditions, at all times of year, and at various times of day and night. The tree lives where it is rooted, unprotected from the elements, in all conditions. Trees are physically linked to the land as their roots search far into the soil for nourishment, building a deep spiritual relationship with the land that feeds and nourishes them. This is the goal for which we should be striving. The whole Celtic system is based upon the individual establishing, maintaining, and developing a physical, mental, and spiritual relationship with the land which gave him or her birth, which feeds him or her, and which ultimately receives the dead body to be reconstructed into new life forms. You must observe each tree under as many circumstances as possible to fully know the tree and how it changes and reacts with the weather, the day, the night, and the seasons. Only then will you learn something of its symbiotic relationship with the Earth.

This process will also reveal quite a bit about yourself, as you force yourself out in rain and snow, dark and cold, autumn and winter, as well as sun and warmth, daylight and brightness, and spring and summer. By getting to know the trees, and by building relationships with them, you are getting to know and build a relationship with your Self.

I would suggest that the Working take the form of a simple ritual. This will help you build a pattern of words, actions, and use of tools which will become increasingly powerful and effective. This ritual should involve the use of your Lesser Magical Weapons (the Knife, Wand, Cup, and Stone—see my book, *Glamoury: Magic of the Celtic Green World*, for how to obtain and prepare these tools), and an invocation to the Daghdha (day-a), the god of the trees.

Start by identifying the tree with which you wish to communicate. Read the chapter about the tree, and build in your mind as complete a picture as you can of the physical appearance of the tree and its more subtle aspects, as found in the Word Oghams. Once you have this information readily available at the mental level, you can begin the physical-level Work. This Work will ultimately affect your spiritual level, which in turn will make itself felt in your day-to-day existence. This is when real, practical, and sustainable progress is being achieved.

There are two parts to this Practical Work. One is the simple ritual, and the other is the creation of a set of Ogham sticks. I would suggest that you collect and fashion your Ogham sticks before you go on to the more formal ritual work. Ogham sticks should be made from the wood of each tree, and carved or painted with the appropriate Ogham symbol for that tree as given in the following chapters. A very practical aspect to this is that it will force you to recognize each tree in the wild at the same time you set in your memory the Ogham notch linked to that tree and its wood. There is no need to make these Ogham sticks large or elaborate. In fact, the smaller they are, the better for you who will be carrying them around a lot. A collection of twenty chunky, but beautifully carved, wooden boards is nowhere as practical as a sheaf of neatly cut and carefully notched thick twigs or thin branches.

The function of these Ogham sticks is twofold. One is as a mnemonic device to remind you of all of the aspects, characteristics, and functions of each tree. This is important in ritual, where much symbolism must be called to mind to invoke the power and energy needed. The other function is one of simple divination. By knowing the different aspects and meanings of each tree, and how these change when placed beside other trees, you can build a whole symbol language that can be used to examine problems or situations, or to answer questions.

You may find it more useful and meaningful to compile your own table of correspondences between the various Oghams, based on your personal experience, observation, and understanding. You will find that you can add to this table as you learn more about the subtle aspects of these useful devices.

To start your Ogham stick collection, I would suggest that you look for each tree in the order in which it appears in the following chapters. What you should be looking for is a fallen branch or twig, approximately six inches long, about half an inch in diameter, and not yet starting to decay. Strip away the bark to reveal the wood beneath, place the stick in a dry, warm part of your home in such a position that you can see it as you go about your daily business. A south-facing windowsill is ideal. Leave it there until the wood is completely dry and hard enough to be carved or painted. In the Spring or Summer, when wood has more sap in it, the drying time may be two or three weeks. In Winter and Autumn this drying time will be shorter. Once it is ready, take it from its drying place and hold it in your hands for some time. Mentally and emotionally form a link with not just the little dried twig in your hand, not just the great tree from which it came, but with all of the trees of that species. As you do this, realize that you are forming a link with a life force that is found not only in your little neck of the woods, but in many other places across the globe.

Still your mind and concentrate on the important task that follows—marking your stick with its appropriate Ogham notch. The carving or painting of the notch will take only a few minutes, but do it with commitment, confidence, and while constantly reviewing in your mind what the notch is called, what it symbolizes, and how you are going to use these pieces of wood for very special and important purposes. Once it has been marked and charged with your thoughts and feelings, put it away in a place special or sacred to you. An altar, if you have one, or a box kept for holding precious belongings is perfect. Repeat this process with each tree until you have a full set of twenty Ogham woods and notches.

You will not be able to find six-inch long, half-inch diameter pieces of ivy, heather, vine, or broom. For these trees, it is perfectly acceptable to use a neutral wood, such as beech or chestnut, and carve or paint them with the appropriate symbol for the tree you wish it to represent. It is the intention behind these chunks of wood that is important. As long as you are clear in your mind what they represent to you and to the Green World, then you have achieved your objective.

The use of these Ogham sticks will be discussed later. For now, spend time identifying trees, collecting twigs, and drying and marking them. You may also consider making a set of three extra sticks, or rather, combinations of sticks. You will remember that the manuscripts describe three double letters: Queirt, nGetal, and Straiph. These double letters could each be represented by three Ogham sticks bound together. Queirt would be a twig of apple for Queirt, plus hazel and heather for C and U. nGetal would be a strip of broom, plus ash and ivy to represent the composite letters N and G. Straiph would be a twig of blackthorn, and its composite letters willow for S, and either oak or holly for D or T.

The Tree Ritual

Using the tip of your Knife, draw a circle in a clockwise direction around your chosen tree, large enough to accommodate both the tree and yourself. Start in the eastern quarter and leave your Knife at that quarter when you have completed the circle. Repeat the process with your Wand, starting at the southern quarter. Leave your Wand at the southern quarter and begin again with your Cup from the western quarter. Leave it at the western quarter and, finally, repeat the process with your Stone starting and finishing in the northern quarter. As you describe these overlapping circles on the ground, be aware of binding yourself to the tree with invisible cords of light. Realize that you are becoming a part of the tree for the duration of your stay within the circle.

If it is not possible to draw a circle big enough to accommodate both you and the tree, or if it is impossible to move completely around the tree because of some obstruction, you can still describe the circle on the ground around yourself, immediately beside the chosen tree, and take into that circle with you a branch, twig, leaf, or fruit of the tree. The point of this sequence is to establish a defined area of ground upon which you will be Working with the tree.

Take the Ogham stick for the tree and focus on it, letting it become your center of attention for a few minutes. This will help your mind concentrate on the tree and remove the distraction of other trees, plants, or wildlife. It also helps the tree to focus on you. Use this time to tune in to the collective knowledge of the thousands of people who have gone before to understand and use the magic of the trees.

When you are ready, hold your Ogham stick in your right hand and push it gently halfway into the ground. Keep hold of the part still above ground, and place your left hand against the trunk of the tree. What you are doing is making your body a physical bridge between the tree and the ground which nourishes and sustains it. It is true, of course, that the tree already has a complex root structure that does this but, on a magical level, you are becoming a root through which the tree can communicate in a natural way. If the ground is too hard or too knotted with roots to allow you to push in the stick, then lay it on the surface of the earth, keeping hold of one end.

Do not expect instant results. Trees grow at a much slower rate than we do, and their whole mental process is on a much slower and more sedate level. Give the tree time to be aware of your fast-moving, flighty intentions. Try to relax physically and mentally, and start to feel the speed at which the tree is moving and evolving. Either internally or aloud, ask the great guardian of trees, the Daghdha, to help you in what you are about to do. The wording of this request is entirely up to you, and should change with each tree to suit that tree's particular meanings and associations. Give some thought to this before you begin each tree exercise. Are there any other characters or deities mentioned in the legends in connection with the tree in question? Do you feel you would also like to ask them for assistance and guidance? As always with such things, go with your feelings, pay attention to your intuition, and do and say what *feels* best, not what you *think* is best.

At this point, some of you may find communication comes easily, and you may enter into a full dialogue with the tree spirit. Others may find that very little seems to happen. This is perfectly normal, and only serves to remind us that we are all different, with different capabilities and strengths—exactly like trees. You will develop at your own natural rate; you cannot force it. Be patient, but be persistent; and keep in mind that you will relate better to some trees than others and, similarly, some trees will relate better to you.

Whatever happens, strong or weak, clear or muddled, make careful note of it in a diary kept exclusively for this purpose. As the months progress, you should start to see a pattern in your Practical Work as noted in your diary. You may find that communication is affected by weather, time of day or night, or time of year. As a rule of thumb, you may find that trees are easier to communicate with in the spring when they are active and their sap is rising than when they are dormant in winter. Whatever you find, take your time, listen carefully, and never prejudge what is going to happen or what you are going to learn. Open your Otherworld eyes, ears, and heart, and let the tree spirit communicate in whatever manner it finds easiest.

Once you have finished each session, thank the tree spirit, even if nothing appeared to happen, thank the Daghdha and anyone else you invoked, and slowly lift your Ogham stick from the ground. As you do, consider that you have now broken contact with the tree and those invoked for aid. Carefully redraw each circle in a counter-clockwise fashion, removing each Magical Weapon as you do so. This frees the tree from its temporary binding with you, and helps you return to the faster moving, mundane world of people, thoughts, and actions. Be prepared; this can be quite a shock to the system after a deep session with a tree spirit. The conscious and deliberate removal of your Working area helps to cushion the blow.

These are the basics for the Practical Work, and should be followed for each tree. Some changes will be made to this ritual when relevant, but do not try to leap ahead by skipping this important step with each tree. There are no shortcuts when it comes to magic, especially slow-moving tree magic.

CHAPTER FIVE

BIRCH

Name: Beithe

Letter: B

Ogham letter: T

Textual reference: Now Beithe has been named from the Birch owing to its resemblance to the trunk of that tree. Of withered trunk, fair-haired the Birch.

Word Ogham of Morainn: FEOCHAS FOLTCHAIN, faded trunk and fair hair.

Word Ogham of Cuchulain: MAISI MALACH .i. CRECCAD, browed beauty, worthy of pursuit.

Word Ogham of Aonghus: GLAISEM CNIS, most silver of skin.

Physical Level

There are two types of birch, the silver birch and the downy birch. The silver birch, with its drooping branches and straight, silvery-white trunk, is a very distinctive tree indeed. It can grow to fifty feet in height, and reaches higher up hillsides than any tree other than the rowan. The small leaves are on alternate sides of the stalk and are thin and shiny with ragged edges, but with a straight base adjoining the stem. The tree produces purple male catkins, with smaller, green, female catkins. These come out around April, and often stay on the tree right through to the start of winter, at which time they break into scales and winged seeds and are carried off by the wind. The wood is unusual, showing no difference between the inner heartwood and the outer sapwood.

The downy birch can grow as high as eighty feet. Its bark is usually red, and its branches do not droop like the silver birch, but tend to be twisted. The leaves and stalks of the downy birch are hairy underneath, with less ragged teeth and a triangular base. Its light leaves are carried far by the wind and rot easily, giving the ground much nutrition. This fertilizing aspect of the dying leaves helps other trees, such as oak and beech, to establish themselves where they might not have otherwise. The effect of this is that the oaks and beeches soon grow taller than the birch, and eventually kill it off by depriving it of light. So, the birch is both a colonizer, or breaker of new ground, and a tree which sacrifices itself for the benefit of others.

Birch woods help to sustain a variety of other life forms. Birds such as the redpoll and tit feed on its seeds. The mottled umber moth caterpillar eats its leaves. Heather and bilberry thrive on the acid-rich soil that birch favors. The small leaves cast a light shadow on the ground beneath the tree, which encourages grasses and other plants to grow. This, in turn, brings rabbits and deer to graze in the birch woods. The bark of the birch is very tough, and survives long after the wood has rotted away, leaving a hollow tube where once had stood a proud tree. Various fungi grow on the dead trees, especially razor strop and bracket fungus on the trunk, and fly agaric on the roots.

An invigorating tea can be made from steeping half a dozen young birch leaves in a pint of boiled water. This is especially beneficial to people suffering from arthritic and rheumatic conditions. Be careful, though, as it will cause frequent urination. A beneficial side-effect of this is that it breaks down kidney and bladder stones. It is a powerful antiseptic which can clear up infections in these regions. It is also a good antiseptic mouthwash for those suffering from mouth ulcers. An inhalation made from hot water and a handful of birch leaves is very good for clearing a blocked nose or stubborn catarrh.

Birch wine can be made from the sugar-rich sap combined with honey. A few tender leaves added to brewing beer afford an extra bite to the taste. The sap is a natural shampoo, and the oil of the bark is an insect repellent. All in all, the birch is a very useful and medicinal tree.

There are several places in Scotland and Ireland that take their names from the Gaelic word for the birch, such as Beith and Cowdenbeath in Scotland. The common Scottish surnames MacBeith, MacBeth, or MacBeath, also come from the word for the birch.

The description in the Word Ogham of Morainn, "faded trunk and fair hair," is no more than a poetic description of the tree's silvery bark and delicate leaves. Even today, it is a great pleasure to stroll through a wild birch wood and enjoy the calm beauty of these delicate trees.

Mental Level

The birch has been placed at the start of the Tree Ogham as a tree of new beginnings and opportunities. To say that any work, magical or mundane, must start with its own beginning is an obvious statement, but this split second in time is extremely important, and should be recognized for what it is. From a magical point of view, when you commence any magical or Otherworld Work, you unconsciously put yourself into a different frame of mind at the very moment you form the idea to do the Work. Recognizing this subtle change in consciousness when it happens is very important; it is an opportunity to make a statement of our intentions behind the magic about to be Worked. We may also carefully consider how to achieve the magic. This mental preparation will be recognized by those in the Otherworld who may be willing to assist us. This is a way of saying plan ahead. It is realizing a very real change within yourself as you give birth to a new idea. This is the deeper meaning in the birch tree's physical attribute of colonizer and starter of new things on the physical level, which can be used during Otherworld journeys as a signifier of new areas of Work or new contacts about to be made. In the Old Irish legend, *Toruigheacht Dhiarmada Agus Ghrainne,* "the Pursuit of Diarmaid and Grainne," the first tree named is a birch, which heralds many magical adventures.

It is good technique to begin your Otherworld journey from the middle of a small birch wood, to provide a conscious signal to your Otherworld guides that you intend to start some new Work. Envision yourself awakening in the Otherworld at dawn, in the center of a small clearing surrounded by young birch trees. Feel the freshness and newness of the day. Feel the vitality and eagerness coursing through your body as you awaken to this new Otherworld day. Realize the potential for change and new beginnings that each dawn brings. Spend a moment studying the birch trees, feeling their presence and vitality. Be aware that, as you move out of the little clearing, you are taking the first steps in this Otherworld setting, and the first steps into a whole new area of Work that will one day manifest in the physical level.

Should a birch tree, or birch wood, crop up spontaneously during a Working, it is an indication that something or someone in the Otherworld is about to make a new contact or start a new area of Work of which you may not have been aware. It is not only you who will think up new things to do on a mental or spiritual level; sometimes the inhabitants of the Otherworld decide that something needs to be done on a physical level, and they may well call upon you for assistance. One way they will bring this to your attention is by gently guiding you to a place of birch trees during an Otherworld journey. Communication between the people of this world and the people of the Otherworld can be very difficult, especially if the communication is initiated by the Otherworld. You must be on the watch for such attempts. The Tree Ogham, as you will see, is probably the best means of Otherworld communication there is.

One of the Gaelic names for birch is *slat chaoil*, which literally means "wand of twigs." The birch is, in fact, a good wood to use for making a magical wand, and this ties in with the tree's importance as a symbol of new beginnings. The wand symbolizes the will of the magician. It is only by the exercising of the will that things get done or that new things get started.

The descriptions given in the Word Oghams of Morainn and Aonghus, "faded trunk and fair hair," and "most silver of skin," can be read on a purely physical level, as the bark is silvery and does appear to flake off and give the trunk a faded or withered look. Its bright leaves in the summer sun do give it a lovely head of fair hair, but there is a deeper meaning to this when you read it as a statement of the birch's self-sacrificing and life-giving properties. Its own trunk dies and fades away, but its leaves fall and enrich the ground, encouraging other stronger trees to take its place. Although this appears to be no more than a physical-level act, it is a very deep and powerful act of magic on all three levels.

Spiritual Level

The name for the birch in the Tree Ogham, *Beithe,* has two meanings in Irish. It can mean "being," in the sense of the verb to be, and it is also a noun meaning, "a being," in the sense of an entity or life force. From a spiritual point of view, the birch is a symbol for the ideal toward which you should be Working—a state where you are prepared to give up that which is your own to help the common good. It is a symbol of being totally unselfish and caring for the needs of others through preparations that help others flourish.

The birch's place at the start of the Tree Ogham serves to set everything else in motion and in its correct order. Throughout the cycle of life, death, and rebirth, it is a tree of physical sacrifice, which brings forth new life that will regenerate itself and place it back at the beginning of things.

I would suggest that, until you are familiar with the Tree Ogham as a whole and with how the trees interact with each other, you confine a deep examination of the birch to the physical and mental levels. Work with birch wood and get to know the feel of the birch by sitting under its branches, with your back against its trunk, while quietly opening your mind to its influences. It is impossible for me to say how you will feel when consciously tuning in to the birch, but I encourage you to pursue the Practical Work with enthusiasm for what you will experience. As the Word Ogham of Cuchulain says, the birch is "a browed beauty that is worthy of pursuit."

Practical Work

Locate a birch tree and find a branch suitable for making your Ogham stick. When you have found such a branch, either on the living tree or on the ground, make your intention to use that branch known to the tree. This is most easily achieved by simply stating aloud that you intend to take a part of the tree, that you are going to use that part of the tree for a very specific and dedicated purpose—communication—and that you are grateful to the tree for providing the piece of wood that you need. Do not do any more with the tree itself at this stage. Cut or pick up the piece and take it home. Follow the instructions for making the Ogham stick as described in Chapter Four.

It may take a few days before the Ogham stick is dry enough to be carved or painted but, during that period, you should still pay daily visits to the tree to engender a feeling of love, compassion, and closeness with it. Talk to it. Tell it your intentions. Tell it your aspirations. Ask it if there is anything you can do for it. In other words, set up a dialogue exactly as you would when making a new human acquaintance.

When your Ogham stick is ready, begin the ritual detailed earlier. Take particular care during this ritual; the birch is the tree of beginnings, and this is your beginning attempt at tree magic. Be aware of this very subtle but important link. This will also be the first time you call upon the Daghdha for assistance. To do this successfully, you should visualize him, perhaps as described in the ancient legend, the "Battle of Moytura," or in my book, *The Irish Celtic Magical Tradition*. The Daghdha is a very large, unkempt, rather rough-looking man, with a big belly, a massive head of tangled, dark hair, and clothes befitting a poor peasant or laborer. His deep, dark eyes shine and betray his soft, gentle, and helpful nature. When you have a clear image of the Daghdha, address him in a manner such as:

> *Oh mighty Daghdha, the Good God, the God of Animals and Forest, Controller of the powers and energies of the Green World, hear me and aid me.*
>
> *It is my deep desire to learn.*
>
> *It is my deep desire to serve.*
>
> *It is my deep desire to obtain knowledge that I can use in this world to help and assist myself and all those of my kind and other kinds who are in need of care and assistance.*
>
> *Guide me through the magical forest of Ogham trees.*
>
> *Reveal to me what lies beneath the bark, teach me what causes the leaves to grow in the shapes which they do, help me understand what causes one tree to be tall and slim, yet another to be short and thick.*
>
> *Show me how to use this knowledge in my daily life that all may benefit from it.*

*Make known to me the link which this tree has with
the earth, with the provider and sustainer of all life,
so that I, too, can nurture such a link.*

Reveal to me, in good time, all that I need to know.

Think over your words for a moment after you have said them.
Visualize the Daghdha coming toward you through a thick forest of
birch. See him standing between you and the tree, in the area you
will occupy when you have pushed your Ogham stick into the
ground and placed your left hand on the tree. Start drawing the
circles on the ground with your Magical Weapons, and follow
through with the rest of the ritual.

This simple ritual will have more of an effect than you may at
first realize. Its strength lies in repetition. The more you perform it,
and the more other people perform it, the stronger it gets; and as it
gets stronger, you will find that you can connect more easily with
the trees. For some people, this will be a very conscious, active, and
revealing experience. For others, it will be a slow, confusing, and
muddled affair. It is difficult to still your mind sufficiently to allow
totally new ways of thinking, feeling, and communicating to take
over, but this is what you must do. By using your circle, and by
calling upon certain helpers and guides, you make this process
easier for yourself and for the tree. Whatever you do, and whatever
happens, don't expect miracles! Rely on slow, steady, and persistent
Work to achieve results. What you are doing is an act of faith; a
spiritual, religious act. Regard it as worship, as deep, spiritual communication between yourself, the spirit of the trees, and the deity or
deities invoked.

When you are finished, before redrawing the circles and removing your Magical Weapons, pull your Ogham stick out of the
ground, hold it in front of you, and say:

Mighty Daghdha, thank you for coming forth to assist and guide me.

I ask that you charge this stick with the knowledge and power of the birch that I may take it with me and use it as a link between myself, the tree, and your good self.

I shall be aware of you, as I know you shall be aware of me, as I go about my daily business.

Return now to the wilds of the forest with my thanks and appreciation.

CHAPTER SIX

ROWAN

Name: Luis
Letter: L
Ogham letter: ᚈ

Textual reference: Luis is named from Mountain Ash as it is the old Gaelic name for rowan. Delight of eye is Mountain Ash owing to the beauty of its berries.

Word Ogham of Morainn: LI SULA, delight of eye.

Word Ogham of Cuchulain: LUTH CETHRA .i. LEAM strength (or friend) of cattle, the elm.

Word Ogham of Aonghus: CARAE CEATHRA, friend of cattle.

Physical Level

The rowan tree is known as the quicken tree or the mountain ash, although it is not a true member of the ash family. It earned this name due to its ability to grow high on mountainsides, clinging precariously to outcrops of rock and fissures in boulders. The general shape of its leaves resembles that of the ash, and hence the name mountain ash. Most people will be familiar with this very attractive and distinctive tree, with its slender shape and clusters of bright red berries. The rowan can grow to sixty-five feet, but is usually quite a bit smaller. Its bark is smooth and shiny gray, with little pores all over it. Its leaves are stalkless and in pairs, long and thin with forward-pointing teeth. In May, it is covered with clusters of little white flowers, which gradually turn into the familiar red berries, a favorite food of many birds.

These berries are edible, but have a very bitter taste, and are best cooked with other fruits to make them palatable. This combination can be made into pies or jelly. The berries can also be boiled for wine. They contain vitamin C and were once used as a cure for scurvy. The juice is both antiseptic and astringent, and may be taken internally or externally. The yellow-gray wood of the rowan is strong and flexible, and was commonly used for making tool handles and carvings. It was also used as a substitute for yew in longbows.

It is rare to find a group of rowans large enough to form a forest. If you come across a group of rowans in full bloom, it is a very bold and fetching sight, especially when they bring a splash of scarlet into what is often a rather barren and bleak hillside. There is a species of rowan found only on the Scottish Isle of Arran that is not a hybrid, but is instead a true genus of rowan. This is appropriate because Arran was considered by the Irish Celts to be the physical manifestation of the Otherworld. This gives the island and everything growing on it a strong magical link.

The surnames MacCairthin and MacCarthy come from the old Gaelic for rowan, and literally mean "son of the rowan." Today, Rowan is a common name in English-speaking parts of the world.

Mental Level

The rowan has long been associated with magic and witchcraft, and many rural dwellers use charms and spells involving rowan to ward off evil or to protect cattle from being milked dry by malicious fairies. The word rowan may come from the old Norse word *runa*, which means "charm" or "spell." Its name in the Tree Ogham, *Luis*, means "swarm" or "a great many." This may be a reference to its plentiful berries, but it could also be a hint of a magical aspect. In the old legends, a rowan tree is often mentioned as an assembly point for warriors. In the great collection of poems known as *Duanaire Finn* (*Lays of Fionn*), there is a lengthy poem called "The Rowan-Tree of Clonfert," which is about a large gathering of the Fianna under a rowan tree.[1] In another of these poems, "The Wry Rowan," two thousand huntsmen gather on a hillside covered in rowan trees.

When rowan appears in Celtic legend, it is mostly in connection with either the druids or some other practitioners of magic. In the great collection of tales known as the *Dindsenchas* (*The History of the Names of Places*), there is mention of a female druid called Dreco, who was the granddaughter of a great male druid called Cartan, whose name was a corruption of Caerthann, which means rowan. Dreco is credited with the wounding of a man called Cethern, using a spear of rowan—a "forked branch of the harsh rowan." Dreco chanted incantations as she dealt the wounding blow, which shows that the rowan was more of a Magical Weapon than an ordinary assault weapon.

It is known that the druids had a special platform, called the Wattles of Knowledge, which was made from interwoven rowan twigs. This was used as a bed during the ritual known as *Tarbh Fheis* (tarv aysh). We do not know much about this ritual other than that the outcome seems to have been a magical trance during which the druid gained hidden knowledge. Druids kindled fires made entirely of rowan before important battles. They used these magical bonfires as a focus for their incantations, in an effort to make the fight go well for their people. In the legend concerning the death of Cuchulain, whose name means Hound of Culain, the Ulster hero is tricked into eating dog's flesh, which he was prohibited from doing because the dog was his totem animal. He knew that to take the dog

---

[1] The Fianna were a group of legendary roving Irish warriors, under the command of Fionn mac Cumhaill, who were an early police force protecting the people during the summer months from Bealtaine to Samhain. The people, by way of payment, billeted them in their homes during the winter.

meat would herald his death, but he was in a position where he could not honorably refuse. The witches who tricked him were roasting the meat on spits of rowan.

The word *luis* also means "herb," which seems odd unless there are medicinal aspects of the bark, sap, leaves, or juices. Herbalists may wish to examine the rowan to establish any useful properties that may have been long forgotten. The same word may stem from a root meaning "flame." Some commentators have taken this to be a poetic reference to the tree's bright berries. If, however, you consider this flame to be the fire that kindles in the mind and soul and produces the divine light of inspiration, you will have a much better image of the tree in connection with its overall magical and druidic associations.

The description given to the rowan in the Word Ogham of Morainn is "delight of eye," and can refer to its pleasing appearance, or to a deeper, more significant meaning. The word, *Li*, actually means "color" or "hue," and not necessarily "delight," as it is usually translated. More importantly, the word *Sula, suil* ("eye" in modern Gaelic), can also mean "expectation," "hope," or "vision." An alternative translation of *Li Sula* could therefore be the "color of vision" or "expectation." Taken on a purely magical basis, this indicates that the rowan may be connected with Otherworld visions, scrying, or divination.

In some versions of the death of Balor, King of the Fomhoire, the hero Lugh is said to have destroyed the evil king's death-dealing eye by throwing a spear of rowan. Note the connection between eyes and rowan. The whole magical aspect of rowan is closely connected with portents of future events and the ability to have Otherworld visions. Its use throughout the centuries in warding off evil spirits and unwanted influences indicates a practical purpose for a wand of rowan, which you might explore.

Spiritual Level

The rowan is closely connected with the Lord of the Hunt, the spirit of the animals and Green World, who appears in many world mythologies under various disguises and names. The most common names are Cernunnos, Herne the Hunter, and under the Irish system, the Daghdha. Our spiritual energies should be channeled toward this image when Working with the rowan. The descriptions given to the tree in the Word Oghams of Cuchulain and Aonghus, "friend of cattle" and "strength of cattle," enforce this connection with the Lord of the Hunt, who sustains and provides for the cattle and all the creatures of the Green World. Cattle were probably chosen for these references due to the great importance of cattle to the ancient Celts. Many of the legends known as *Tana* (raids) center on cattle raids, such as the epics *Tain Bo Cuailnge* ("Cattle Raid of Cooley") and *Tain Bo Fraoch* ("Cattle Raid of Fraoch").

The Lord of the Hunt is always depicted as being fierce, ugly, and aggressive, with horns and a vicious-looking club. Beneath the surface, he is really a caring, helpful, and docile being, willing to help you, if you are worthy. He is one of the great Openers of the Way who will test intruders in his world, but who will also direct the frightened traveler to safety and along the road to fulfillment.

In the "Pursuit of Diarmaid and Grainne," the two lovers hide in a rowan tree that grew from a berry brought to Ireland from *Tir Tairngire* (the Land of Promise), a poetic name for the Otherworld. This tree is protected by a fearsome character called Searbhan Lochlannach, which means "Servant of Norway." Norway is another poetic allusion to the Otherworld. He is described in this passage:

> A thick-boned swarthy giant and weapons do not wound
> him and fire does not burn him and water does not drown
> him, and there is only one eye on the top of his forehead.
> There is a thick collar of iron round the body of the giant

79

and an iron club through the end of the collar and the collar is wound round the body of the giant. He is not doomed to die until three strokes of his own club are struck on him; and he sleeps on the top of the rowan tree by night and at its foot by day guarding it. He has made a wilderness of the area around him and the Fianna of Ireland do not dare chase or hunt there for fear of him.[2]

This is a typical description of the Lord of the Hunt in mythology. The rowan's ability to impart Otherworld knowledge is shown later in the same legend, when Fionn and his warriors make camp at the foot of the tree. To pass the time, Fionn plays a game known as *fidchell*, which was similar to chess. This word means "wood-knowledge," which implies that, to play it successfully, one had to be conversant with the trees and, perhaps, fluent in Tree Ogham. In the legend, Fionn's opponent is about to be defeated, but Diarmaid, who is high in the tree above them watching the game with interest, sees a way out of the situation. He drops one of the rowan's berries onto the *fidchell* piece the opponent should move next. The player does this, and eventually wins the game. It was, symbolically, the rowan which gave him the knowledge to win.

The Lord of the Hunt represents the two sides of the Green World that must be recognized and accepted by those of this world who wish to live in harmony with it. There is the harsh, threatening, and uncontrollable Nature, but there is also a softer, gentler, more pacific side seen in the beauty of the plants and folds of the earth, the stillness of a summer's day full of the hum of insects, the delight of a cow with calf, sheep with lamb, and mother with baby. Both of these aspects are necessary, and it is only our reactions to them that makes one different from the other.

The Lord of the Hunt will help you to understand this, and face up to both of these aspects in your dealings with the powers and

---

[2] Gerard Murphy, trans., *Duanaire Finn* (Dublin: The Irish Texts Society, 1954).

energies of the Green World. Although he is an ugly, frightening character who issues grave threats, warnings, and challenges, at this level, he should be seen as the Higher aspect of your Self, which can also appear hideous or frightening during magical Workings.

The rowan is the second tree of the Tree Ogham, yet it is the highest tree in that it climbs higher up the mountainside than any other, in search of illumination. When it succeeds and puts down roots to grow, its bright red berries shine like a beacon from the greenness of its mountain home, encouraging the weary traveler to make that final effort to reach the top. This is a good image to keep in mind when dealing with the rowan on a spiritual level.

Work with the rowan as often as possible throughout the four seasons to understand the subtle way it changes, and how you react to these changes, as the year is born, grows, wanes, dies, and is reborn. Work with it over the changes of the year to highlight the different aspects of the Green World as the seasons come and go. Discover this aspect of your own nature: How do you feel about visiting the Green World during winter as well as summer? On cold, wet days as well as warm, calm ones? In morning and evening? When you are fit and well, and when you are tired and hungry? These, too, are the two aspects of the Lord of the Hunt, and also of yourself. You must experience these things to understand yourself and your place in the Green World.

Practical Work

The Daghdha is more closely connected with the rowan than with the birch, but this is not a concern right now. For the time being, he will serve as a guide and teacher for all of the trees. Once you work your way through all twenty, you can reexamine the more subtle links between the trees and the deities you encounter along the way.

Carry out the tree ritual described earlier and, as you call upon the Daghdha each time, try to determine if he appears differently, or feels different from when you first encountered him while Working with the birch. As you progress, you will realize that the way he reveals himself, and the information he imparts, is geared to the aspects of each tree. Being aware of this may help to clear up confusion when this changing aspect becomes more noticeable.

This would be a good time to make yourself a Wand of rowan, to be used for ritual Workings of a very magical nature, or for Workings that require more assistance and protection than normal. An ideal length for such a Wand is between twelve and fifteen inches; any larger becomes cumbersome, and any smaller may become confused with your Ogham sticks. It is best to make a rowan Wand from a piece of the living tree. Some people consider it improper to cut pieces off living trees, but I feel that living wood is best, because it encapsulates the vital energies of the tree and makes the Wand more effective. It is vital, however, to first explain to the tree what you are going to do and why. I personally do not decorate my Wands, but if you feel some designs, words, or symbols are appropriate and have meaning to you, then by all means use them. Once your Wand has been cut, stripped of bark, and dried, you should dedicate it as described in my book, *Glamoury: Magic of the Celtic Green World*. Keep your Wand with your Ogham sticks and other Magical Weapons to be used during rituals that are new to you, or when you feel pressure and need extra assistance.

Continue the exercises with the rowan until you are satisfied with your progress. Remember to keep a written record in your magical diary of what happened or didn't happen during the Working, and of any ideas, feelings, or coincidences that occur during your day-to-day life. These can be just as revealing as anything imparted to you during formal magical Workings.

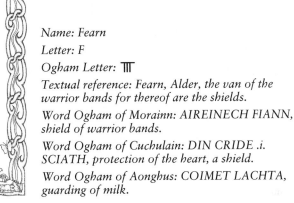

CHAPTER SEVEN

ALDER

Name: Fearn

Letter: F

Ogham Letter: ᚗ

Textual reference: Fearn, Alder, the van of the warrior bands for thereof are the shields.

Word Ogham of Morainn: AIREINECH FIANN, shield of warrior bands.

Word Ogham of Cuchulain: DIN CRIDE .i. SCIATH, protection of the heart, a shield.

Word Ogham of Aonghus: COIMET LACHTA, guarding of milk.

Physical Level

The alder tree is a very ancient tree that has grown in the British Isles for thousands of years. It is easily recognized by its regularly spaced branches and its conical shape, growing to a height of up to seventy feet. Its gray bark is rough and often covered in young shoots. Its leaves are round, on alternate sides of the stalk, and sometimes notched at the tip. Alders bear both male and female catkins, the male catkins being considerably longer than the rounded female catkins. It is usually found growing on wet ground and the banks of rivers, where its roots help hold the soil together and bind nitrogen, making the soil more nutrient rich. When it is cut, the wood appears a blood-red color, turning yellow when seasoned. Because of this bleeding effect, the tree was looked upon as evil by early woodsmen. Dyes can be obtained from the bark, the fruit, and the leaves. A distillation of the leaves or bark is an excellent remedy for burns and inflammations. The same distillation can be used to alleviate the distressing skin condition of impetigo. The freshly picked leaves are an excellent natural insect repellent, and fleas especially cannot abide their smell. The wood is good for carving and lasts a long time in water without rotting, making it a popular wood in the construction of jetties, and the ancient Celtic lake dwellings known as *Crannogs*, which required deeply sunk, long-lasting piles.

Mental Level

It is clear from the various textual references that warriors' shields were made from alder wood, although aspen was also much in favor for this purpose. This was due to alder's toughness, which could withstand hard blows yet at the same time be easy to work with. Its bloody appearance when first felled may also have influenced the shieldmaker's choice.

Weapons were often given names by the Celts, and quite often were credited with magical powers. In a passage from the "Cattle Raid of Cooley," there is a section which describes King Conchobhar mac Neasa's palace. Within this palace was one special room set aside to house the shields of the warriors when they were not at war:

> Conchobhar's four gold bordered shield Ochain was there; Cuchulain's black shield Duban; Conall Cernach's Swift Lamthapad; Ochnech that was Flidais's; the red-gold of Orderg that was Furbaide's; Ecgtach the Death Dealing that was Amargin's; Condere's angry Ir; The Bright Torch of Cainnel that was Nuadhu's; Uathach The Fearful that was Dubthach's; Errge's Lettach; Menn's Brattach; The Happy

Luithech that was Noisiu's; Sencha's loud Sciatharglan;
Comla Catha, the Door of Battle that was Celtchar's.[1]

The title given to the alder in the Word Ogham of Morainn, *Aireinech Fiann,* "shield of warrior bands," is clearly appropriate on the mundane level. It should be noted, however, that *Aireinech* does not mean a physical shield, but means "to protect" or "take care of." What the text is really saying is that it was not so much the physical wooden shields that protected the warrior bands, but the spirit of the tree itself. This protective quality of alder can still be used today, despite the fact that we no longer need to carry shields of alder wood. When we feel threatened, we can invoke the spirit of the alder, using our knowledge of its spiritual aspects to aid us. Beware, however, of thinking that a deep knowledge of magical associations is all you need to get out of dangerous situations; you must still use the same methods and resources of this world as would anyone else in similar circumstances. The difference for you is that you are aware of higher forces at work for your benefit and safety.

The other names given in the Word Oghams of Aonghus and Cuchulain, "guarding of milk" and "protection of the heart, that is a shield," also reflect the protecting qualities of the alder on a level higher than the physical. To guard milk may sound a bit odd, but if you consider the great value, both material and spiritual, placed on cattle by the Celts as well as the great nourishing properties of the milk of cattle, it becomes clear how important this role would have been. Similarly, to protect the heart, as opposed to the whole body, implies a deeper purpose as well.

You might ask what, at this enlightened level, could threaten you, and from what might you need protection? In most people's minds, the spiritual level is a place of peace and harmony, above

---

[1] Cecile O'Rahilly, *Tain Bo Cuailgne* (Dublin: Irish Texts Society, 1962).

threats and violence. Unfortunately, this is not the case. There is as much danger, evil, and threat to your well-being on the spiritual level as on the physical. We shall look at this important point in more detail as we progress through the Tree Ogham.

Alder's place is at the front of battle, as the shield goes before the warrior. This suggests a courageous aspect as well as a protective one; and herein lies a hint as to its properties and uses on a magical level. If you are caught up in one of those Otherworld journeys that takes on a life of its own, where things get out of hand, or you feel you are losing control, then imagining yourself going boldly forward while carrying a shield of alder wood can help invoke the protection of the spirit of the alder, and set things back on a more controllable course. It is important to know that the alder is protective only when you are on the defensive. If you try to go forward carrying an alder shield in an offensive state, it is unlikely you will get the protection you think you are entitled to, and you could find yourself worse for the wear.

There is a place for aggression in the Otherworld (remember that this whole system was developed by a warrior people), but the real skill of the warrior is knowing when to be aggressive and when not to be, knowing when to take up the sword and when to take up the shield. We shall deal with the attributes of the warrior when they occur in our study of the Tree Ogham. For the moment, it should suffice to say that the alder is a tree of Otherworld protection.

Spiritual Level

The spiritual essence of the alder is in going forth, in taking up a challenge and stepping forward boldly and bravely, prepared to tackle whatever is thrown at you. It was said earlier that the birch is the tree of new beginnings; the rowan is the tree of facing up to the things about yourself and your place in the Green World; and now the alder is the tree to take up once the tests of the rowan have been accepted and overcome. It is a tree of confident continuation. You may now be seeing the deliberate order in which the trees of the Tree Ogham have been set, and that the experiences of one are used as a base upon which the next can build. You may also see why it is vital that you fully experience and understand each tree before moving on to an examination of the next.

The alder's advancing aspect is of the utmost importance, for it is only by breaking new ground, by making ourselves face up to things we have previously avoided, that we can ever progress. This takes courage and a willingness to accept hardships and failure, but the blows can be softened on the spiritual level by the careful use of an alder shield. During Otherworld journeys, this can be accomplished by visualizing yourself carrying a shield strapped to your forearm, in front of your heart, as you boldly stride into unknown and hostile territory with confidence that your shield will protect you. You must also wear this shield on a spiritual level, but this can only be done once you have managed to experience for yourself the alder's unique spirit.

Because it is a tree most useful on the physical level when half submerged in water, it is a good symbol of the state in which an active magician should be: constantly aware of things both above and below the surface, and a safe and secure foundation upon which to build new and useful structures. Meditations on these mental and spiritual aspects of the alder will prove fruitful and, during times of stress or tension, helpful and soothing.

Practical Work

Keep in mind all of the images and ideas described in the last paragraph while carrying out the Ogham stick and tree rituals associated with the alder. Pay particular attention to the protecting aspect of the Daghdha when you ask for his assistance. By evoking this aspect of the Daghdha, you will make yourself more aware of what this really means as an aspect of the tree. You should also consider this protecting aspect more carefully when describing your circles on the ground with your Magical Weapons. Just as they are the limitations of your Working area, they are also protective barriers between you and anything which may try to interfere with your Work and progress.

You may wish to consider constructing an alder Shield while carrying out this exercise. This does not need to be a solid, round, thick, or heavy artifact. It is quite acceptable to make a Shield from an interlacing of alder twigs and branches shaped roughly into a circle. As is always the case with Magical Weapons, it is what they symbolize that is important, not how they look physically or artistically. After you have constructed and dedicated your Shield, you can use it as an aid to invoke help and guidance during Workings.

As always, take careful note of what you hear and what you see. Once you are confident that you have learned as much as you can from the alder, progress to the next tree in our *Beithe Luis Nion* sequence.

CHAPTER EIGHT

WILLOW

Name: Sail

Letter: S

Ogham letter: ⁤ℼ

Textual reference: Sail, Willow, the color of a lifeless one, owing to the resemblance of its color to a dead person.

Word Ogham of Morainn: LI AMBI, hue of the lifeless.

Word Ogham of Cuchulain: TOSACH MELA .i. SAIL, beginning of loss, Willow.

Word Ogham of Aonghus: LUTH BEACH, strength of bees.

Physical Level

The willow is usually found along river banks, and can grow to a height of sixty feet. It is an imposing sight with its thick trunk covered in dark gray, heavily ridged bark, and its spreading branches creating a very full shape. Its leaves are long and slender, on alternate sides of the stalk, and covered in silver hairs that give the whole tree a shimmering appearance. The long, yellow, male catkins appear in early spring, and the green, female catkins appear about the same time, but on separate trees. The female catkins produce fluffy seeds that are easily caught up and carried away by the wind.

Willow wood is used for a variety of purposes. Its long, thin stems are most useful for making fences, baskets, lobster pots, and so on. The maturing trees are pollarded, which means the top of the tree is cut off in order to encourage more branches to appear. The young shoots grow long and straight, and can be cut back to provide the thin but strong poles and rods needed in the manufacture of the goods mentioned above. Osier, a smaller species of willow, is similarly used, but it is coppiced as opposed to pollarded. This means it is cut down to ground level to encourage a mass of long, straight stems to grow.

It is known that the Irish Celts practiced both pollarding and coppicing of willow and osier to provide material for not only baskets and chairs, but also for the wattle walls of their houses. Wattling was a technique where a double wall of willow rods was woven and the gap between the outer and inner walls was filled with earth to provide a strong, wind- and water-tight wall. So tightly were these walls woven that they did not require any additional sealant for protection. Archaeological excavations have revealed houses made in this way whose walls required five miles of willow rods to make, suggesting that an advanced system of tree harvesting must have been in use during Celtic times. This harvesting of willow is still carried on in some regions today.

The wood, bark, and leaves of the willow have a variety of useful medicinal purposes, and it is a tree worth cultivating for this alone. The bark contains a chemical that is the source of aspirin, a good analgesic. This chemical is known to decrease sexual desire when taken internally, but it is also a useful drug for cases of spermatorrhea. Conversely, a concoction made from the leaves or sap, if applied externally to the sexual organs, can increase sexual ability. (Could this be what the Word Ogham of Morainn was suggesting as the "hue of the lifeless"?) A weak solution of sap or crushed leaves is an excellent gargle for those suffering from nasal or sinusal catarrh, and can also be used as a soothing eye lotion. A stronger preparation of leaves is an effective shampoo for dandruff, flaking skin, spots, and blemishes. It is a good styptic, which can stop minor bleeding without much difficulty.

Mental Level

The willow's description in the textual references, "color of a lifeless one," does not seem consistent with its many practical and medicinal uses. It may, instead, be a hint at its Otherworld connections, and an indication that it has many uses on an Otherworld level. The expression, *Li Ambi*, literally means "color of not living." This does not specifically mean lifeless or dead, but refers to a state between being alive and being dead. To put it another way, it refers to a form of living other than the one we know and experience in this world. It is, in fact, a reference to the dwellers of the Otherworld.

To the Celts, with their unshakable and total belief in the continuation of life after physical death, a person may have appeared to be dead in this world, but he or she was still very much alive in the Otherworld. To say that the color of the willow tree resembles that of a dead person is, therefore, an allusion to the new life and freedom of the Otherworld. The cycle of death and rebirth is perfectly illustrated by the willow tree itself: annually it is chopped down to the ground, or has its head cut off, springing forth the next year with a great number of new branches. The willow's preference for river banks and fords also gives it an air of being between worlds, as these borders are in-between states, and very important places. Witness the number of battles, magical events, and important decisions described in the legends that take place in fords, at river banks, or on beaches. This is a good image to use during your Otherworld journeys, when you wish to move from one stage of the Working to another, or when you wish to focus your concentration on what is about to unfold.

See yourself arriving at a ford or river bank, and crossing from one side to the other. As you do so, be aware of your concentration increasing and your consciousness rising. Doing this while using the image of a willow tree beside the ford or along the river bank, or while you are carrying a willow basket or a bunch of willow hurdles, will help you tune in to the vibrations of the

Otherworld at this important stage in the Working. This will also give you a physical symbol that the Otherworld forces and beings can recognize and use to help you.

The names given to the willow in the Word Oghams of Aonghus and Cuchulain, "strength of bees" and "beginning of loss," also refer to the willow's Otherworld connections. Bees were considered by the ancient Celts to be from the Otherworld, and their ordered and regimented society was seen as a model upon which human society should be based. This is a good example of the practical way in which the ancient Celts learned from the Green World around them. If they saw something happening in the plant or animal kingdoms that looked useful or instructive, they would do their best to adopt such things into their own lives. Most of us have lost this ability to recognize our true place in the Green World, along with the skill to learn from the plants, animals, birds, fishes, and insects whose movements, habits, and lifestyles contain valuable instruction for us. I hope this study of the trees will help you regain at least part of this lost skill.

The "beginning of loss" refers to the realizations which invariably come upon you when you start to become conscious of the Otherworld and its powers and energies. The effect of this is often that the material things you had craved for so long lose their appeal. Letting go of the ties that bind in this world is one way to start opening up in the Otherworld. You must be prepared to lose in this world to gain in the Otherworld. The beginning of loss is, therefore, a very positive and important step, and one which you must go through if you are ever to progress.

Most of us can immediately think of things we can do without; things which, if we were to be honest with ourselves, are really a hindrance to us. Most of these things will be material objects. The real things you must start to lose are more abstract, such as incorrect attitudes or ideas, bad habits, and incorrect and unhealthy relationships with people and, especially, with the Otherworld.

It will take a long time for most of these to become obvious to you, but if you follow the instructions of the trees, they will become more apparent. This is when the real tests begin. Will you really be able to give up lifelong beliefs or relationships at the drop of a hat (or leaf) just to gain some ill-defined state of advancement? It is very easy to answer yes to this question from a purely hypothetical point of view; however, when the time actually comes, things will suddenly seem very different and far from clear cut. Progressing to the next level of the willow should help with this dilemma.

Spiritual Level

The spiritual essence of the willow is as a foundation, and as the confidence to go forward into the unknown without fear or trepidation. As has already been said, bees were considered to be the perfect image of a structured society, with each individual knowing and understanding his or her part in the whole. The expression, "strength of bees," signifies the strength to be able accept one's place in the scheme of things, and participate.

The long, flexible, willow stems were and still are used in the construction of the Celtic boat called the *coracle*. Willow laid the foundation of the vessel, which would confidently and safely carry its passenger over the waters to new lands. The willow can, therefore, be seen as a continuation of the alder—the building block permanently half submerged in water—which has now become the foundation of the floating craft. The magician, aware of what is both above and below the waters, has now taken up that knowledge, determined to sail forth. You, too, will take the knowledge you have gained and set sail with the help of the willow. Are you ready for this deceptively simple step? Think well on this before you try.

A form of punishment in Celtic society was banishment from the tribe or clan, which was sometimes done by casting the errant adrift in a coracle. The Otherworld forces would then decide if he or she would be carried safely to shore, or if the coracle would be upset and the hapless wrong-doer drowned. The lesson of this tree on the magical level may be to set yourself adrift from society with only the support and guidance of the trees to assist you. The fact that you have decided to follow a magical discipline has already set you apart; if you can take this bold step into the unknown, prepared to face the inevitable, then you will show your true inner strength—the strength of bees. This will attract help and assistance from the Otherworld by those whose task it is to watch out for lone voyagers, and to guide them until they reach their own perfect part of the Otherworld.

Practical Work

Use your tree ritual to gain a deeper understanding and awareness of the properties of the willow within your mind and heart. During the opening invocation to the Daghdha, be aware of another shadowy figure coming through the forest. This will be your personal Otherworld guide and guardian, who will be revealed to you in due time. You will probably find that he or she is a key figure from Celtic mythology, so you may want to prepare by reading as many of the legends as you can. Fill your conscious and unconscious mind with names, images, and details for your guide to call upon during Otherworld journeys, to explain things to you and, ultimately, to make his or her true identity known to you. (See the Bibliography for books that will aid this process.)

You should also understand that this guide will be with you twenty-four hours a day from now on. He or she will use every opportunity to communicate with you, and to guide and assist you. Very often this guidance will come when you least expect it; while you are taking a shower, driving to work, walking the dog, falling asleep, or waking up. Be alert and receptive to make your guide's task easier, and be aware that you now have a guide whom you should include in your opening invocation and closing words of thanks. These words do not need to be formal or set in ritualistic tones, but can be more of a hello and good-bye to an old friend, for this is what your guide will become. Nurture a feeling of closeness and affection rather than a relationship of pupil and teacher.

CHAPTER NINE

ASH

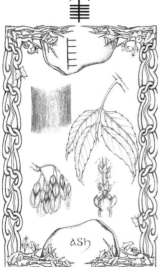

Name: Nion

Letter: N

Ogham letter: ⵑⵑⵑⵑ

Textual reference: Nion, Ash, a check on peace is Nion for of it are made the spear-shafts by which the peace is broken.

Word Ogham of Morainn: COSTUD SIDE, checking of peace.

Word Ogham of Cuchulain: BAG MAISI .i. GARMAN, flight of beauty, a weaver's beam.

Word Ogham of Aonghus: BAG BAN, the flight of women.

Physical Level

The ash can grow to one-hundred-thirty feet high, and is the largest tree we have encountered so far. It has smooth, greenish-gray bark, which starts to crack and open as the tree gets older. Its branches are long and widely spaced. Its leaves are also long, on opposite sides of their stalks, and with each stalk having as many as thirteen leaves. It has distinctive black buds, and its seeds, which are popularly known as ash keys, grow in bunches, each with a long, thin wing.

The ash grows in virtually all climates and conditions, but flourishes in lime-rich soil. It has very long roots that often strangle those of neighboring trees. Its white wood is excellent for burning, and is also strong and pliable for use in oars, ax handles, hockey sticks, and skis. Ash was the favorite wood of the Celts for making spears.

Its medicinal uses are varied. It was believed that a decoction of ash leaves was a good antidote for snake bites (but I don't know how accurate this is, and wouldn't recommend it on its face). The juices and sap are good at relieving conditions related to stones in the bladder, and are also mild appetite suppressants. The leaves are a laxative, and help arthritic and rheumatic conditions. If the leaves are unavailable, such as in the winter, the bark can be used with equal efficacy.

Ash is a common surname among English-speaking peoples.

Mental Level

From descriptions in the legends and from archaeological finds, we know that the Celts preferred ash for making spear shafts, because it grows long and straight and, once hardened in fire, becomes very strong. The spear was an important offensive weapon to the ancient Celts. There are descriptions in the legends of very exotic spears with inlaid shafts, carefully engraved heads, and elaborate thongs attached to them for throwing. Some of the earlier Celtic tribes had tribal names that may have originated from old names for spears.

There is a race of people mentioned in many of the Irish legends who are known as the Fir Bolg. This name is most often translated as "Men (*Fir*) of the Bags (*Bolg*)," but the word *bolg* was also used to describe a type of spear. A possible alternate translation could be "Men of the Spears." There are several legends that describe these warriors as having very superior spears, which makes the title Men of the Spears seem more appropriate than Men of the Bags. Another Irish tribe was called the Gaileoin, which means "Spears (*Gai*) of Wounding (*leoin*)." With the exception of the sling, the spear was the only long-range weapon used by the Irish Celts of the Bronze and Iron Ages.

The spear which will concern us is not the warrior's fighting weapon, but the magician's symbolic weapon—one of the four Greater Magical Weapons. As such, it has more meaning, and is of more use than, an ordinary battle weapon. These four Greater Magical Weapons are described in two important Irish legends, the "Battle of Moytura" and *The Book of the Invasions of Ireland*. (You will not find them described there as Magical Weapons, as this is a modern title.) The Spear in question was the Spear which eventually belonged to Lugh of the Long Arm, one of the more important of the Celtic deities. He got his unusual name from the simple fact that the holder of a spear has a much longer reach than someone without. His Spear was said to have been brought from the Otherworld city of Gorias.

The other three Magical Weapons described are the Sword of Nuadhu, which was brought from the Otherworld city of Findias; the Cauldron, which belonged to the Daghdha and was brought from Murias; and the great Lia Fail, the Stone of Destiny, which was brought from Falias, and which belonged not to a person, but to a place—Tara. In writing, these Magical Weapons appear with an initial capital letter to distinguish them from their lesser, mundane counterparts. (See my book, *Glamoury: Magic of the Celtic Green World*, for a full discussion of the Greater and Lesser Magical Weapons.)

The uses for these Greater Magical Weapons are many, but here we shall concentrate on one aspect of one weapon only—the Spear. By tradition, the Spear equates with the Lesser Magical Weapon of the Wand, which represents the will of the magician. The Spear is a greater and more powerful symbol of the magician's will, and one which should be used during group ritual Workings, or as a severe means of dealing with something on a purely personal level.

During your magical studies, you may find that a period of inactivity develops, a period when you seem to lose the desire to get up and do anything. On the physical day-to-day level, we call it boredom. You must realize that it can occur on the mental and spiritual levels as well. Should this occur, the only way out is to break this enforced peace suddenly and deliberately by taking up arms (your Magical Weapons) and fighting the lethargy. The best weapon to use in these circumstances is the Spear; for it is only the deliberate use of willpower that will overcome inertia, and set you back on your path. This is what is meant by the rather odd description of the ash in the Word Ogham of Morainn: "checking of peace." How you go about this is up to you. You may wish to do it in an Otherworld journey, where you can visualize your inertia and laziness as a hideous figure you must either kill or drive away with your Spear. You may find it more powerful and beneficial to use your Spear in a formal ritual, where you also use your physical body, in itself a beneficial and positive aspect. This "checking of the peace" is not necessarily an aggressive and hostile act. Remember that this system of magic was devised by a warrior race, but we should not let our modern view of war and weapons influence the way we look upon these things.

The other two references in the Word Oghams of Cuchulain and Aonghus, "flight of beauty," and "flight of women," are poetic allusions to this same principle. In the legends, the Otherworld self of the magician, the part that houses the willpower, is often seen as a wise and beautiful woman who comes to advise the magician during crucial points in his or her Workings. Often these female figures appear when nothing is happening but, as a result of their visit, a great deal suddenly begins to happen. The peace has been checked. The flight of the woman or the flight of beauty is the flight of the magician's lethargy.

This phenomenon of inner boredom is often associated with a course of study, when the student comes to a point where initial enthusiasm wanes and further progress becomes difficult. In magical study, this is the stage of the ash tree. The wise men and women who devised this system thousands of years ago placed the ash tree exactly where it would be needed most.

The Word Ogham of Cuchulain also refers to "a weaver's beam," which is a poetic allusion to a spear. These frequent cryptic references in the Irish Celtic legends are known as *kennings*. The dialogue between Cuchulain and Eimhear in Chapter One consists entirely of kennings. When a kenning is used instead of the common name for an object, it is an indication that a more subtle aspect of the object is being suggested. The connection between a weaver's beam and a spear could be obvious, in that both are straight, sharp-pointed, and meant to be pushed or thrown in a straight line. There is also a reference to this in the "Battle of Moytura," which states that one is a kenning for the other. In this legend, Ruadan, a member of the Fomhoire, has come in disguise to the camp of his enemies, the Tuatha De Danann. As he attempts to obtain some of their weapons, his deceit is discovered and he is killed by a throw from a spear; "for that reason a weaver's beam is still called 'the spear of the maternal kin' in Ireland."[1] This kenning will crop up again when we examine the fir later in our study of the Tree Ogham.

Spiritual Level

The word *Nion* comes from a root word meaning "a thing produced." When Working with the ash tree on a spiritual level, the most obvious thing produced is the Spear itself. The essence of the spiritual aspect of ash is to deliberately bring your willpower, symbolized by the Spear, to bear on the spiritual level. Because this level is linked to the other two levels, your willpower will eventually manifest on those other levels as well.

The Irish Celts believed there were five specific trees, located throughout Ireland, which had special properties on a magical and

---

[1] E.A. Gray, trans., *Cath Maige Tuired* (Dublin: Irish Texts Society, 1983). We don't know why the writer made this connection between the spear and the weaver's beam, but he did. This connection crops up in many similar passages in legends.

spiritual level. Because of this, they were used as places of assembly. Three of these five magical trees were ash trees, places for the assembly of warriors, and the other two were yews, for the assembly of druids. A reference in the *Prose Dindsenchas* says that a great man, called Trefuilngid Tre-Ochair, the Three Cornered Strong Upholder, came to Tara one day to settle a dispute about Ireland's history. He carried with him the branch of a tree, signifying he had come from the Otherworld. Upon leaving, he gave the wise sage Fionntan some berries from this branch.

> He left with Fionntan some of the berries from the branch which was in his hand, so that he planted them in whatever places he thought it likely they would grow in Ireland. And these are the trees which grew up from those berries; the ancient tree of Tortu, the tree of Ross, the tree of Mugna, the branching tree of Dathi and the ancient tree of Uisneach.[2]

Another reference to the trees, taken from later in the *Dindsenchas*, says:

> Eo Mugna, great was the fair tree,
>
> High its top above the rest,
>
> thirty cubits—it was no trifle,
>
> that was the measure of its girth.
>
>
> Three hundred cubits was the height of the blameless tree.
>
> Its shadow sheltered a thousand.

---

[2] R.I. Best, trans., *The Settling of the Manor of Tara*, Eriu 4, Part 2 (Dublin, 1923).

In secrecy it remained in the north and east
Until the time of Conn Ceadchathach.

A hundred score of warriors, no empty tale,
Along with ten hundred and forty
Would that tree shelter, it was a fierce struggle,
Until it was overthrown by the poets.

How fell the Bough of Daithi?
It spent the strength of many a gentle hireling.
An ash, the tree of the nimble hosts,
Its top bore no lasting yield.

The ash of Tortiu, take count thereof,
The ash of populous Uisneach.
Their boughs fell, it was not amiss,
In the time of the Sons of Ead Slane.

The Yew of Mugna, it was a hallowed treasure,
Nine hundred bushels was its bountiful yield,
It fell in Dairbre southward,
Across Magh Ailbe of the cruel combats.

The Bole of Ross, a comely yew,
With abundance of broad timber,

The tree without hollow or flaw,

The stately bole, how did it fall?[3]

A further excerpt from the same source adds:

Berries to the berries the Strong Upholder put upon the Ash of Tortiu. Three fruits upon it, namely acorn, apple and nut, and when the first fruit fell another fruit used to grow.[4]

These two trees, the ash of the warrior and the yew of the druid, may be linked in more ways than we first recognize. A very common man's name in Ireland was "Eochaidh," which is often translated as "horse" or "horse warrior," but which can also mean "yew warrior." This name may contain some hidden significance as to the bearer's status as a warrior, not only in the physical sense, but also in a magical sense. This also suggests the status for which we should be striving at this level.

The willow gave us the ability and the confidence to sail forth into our own unknown. Now the ash is giving us the willpower, and the Magical Weapons should we need them, to use our magical abilities to create changes on all three levels. This emphasizes the point that all magic should eventually have a physical-level outcome. The three levels are so interlocked that whatever is done on one level will inevitably have an effect upon the other two. Knowing and using this at a spiritual level will allow you to Work powerful, useful, and effective magic, which will filter down the branches of your ash tree and manifest in the physical world. Likewise, whatever you do in the physical world will affect your mental and spiritual levels. This is another reason I have stressed the importance of getting to know the physical trees in their natural habitats.

---

[3] Edward Gwynn, trans., *The Metrical Dindsenchas* (Dublin: Hodges, Figgis & Co.).
[4] Ibid.

By carrying out such an act on the physical level, you will be bringing knowledge to the mental and spiritual levels.

Now that you have started to use your magical powers, you must prepare for a certain amount of backlash. It is a rule of magic that whenever you start something new, there is inevitably a reaction, which is guaranteed to shake your flimsy little coracle of willow stems. This backlash is symbolized by the next letter of the Tree Ogham.

Practical Work

As well as invoking the Daghdha and your Otherworld guide, you should now also invoke the god Lugh during the basic ritual. Lugh is closely associated with the Spear as a Magical Weapon, and he is the best person to instruct you on when and how to use it. Lugh is usually described in very shining, bright, and dazzling terms. He is a very muscular and young warrior who carries a great ash spear. A suggested invocation for Lugh would be:

> *Shining Lugh of the Long Arm, keeper of the Fiery Spear of Gorias, I salute you and recognize your power and warriorhood.*
>
> *Assist me.*
>
> *Teach me all that I need to know of the ash, of Spears, and of my own ability to go forth to destroy inertia and bring true peace where it is needed.*
>
> *Charge my Ogham stick with these properties.*
>
> *Let it become a symbol of your Fiery Spear.*
>
> *Let me, too, be known as [your name] of the Long Arm.*

Teach me to recognize and control the warrior within me.

Teach me to recognize my true strength and energy in this world and the Otherworld.

Now is a good time to make your own ceremonial Spear of ash, four to five feet long, and as straight as possible. It will take time to find a suitable piece of ash from which to make this Magical Weapon, but this seeking is as much a part of the magical Work as the formal rituals. Go about this task in a magical frame of mind.

It is going to take more effort to cut such a large piece of wood from a living tree (assuming, of course, there are no suitable fallen branches) than it did to make your Ogham stick. Certain practical considerations need to be taken into account: Is taking such a large piece of wood going to damage the tree? This may be the case if you are thinking about using a branch from a very young tree, or from one that has sustained damage and lost limbs already. If you are satisfied that you are not going to do the tree any damage, you must consider whether or not the tree belongs to someone or is on someone's property. Do you have permission to cut a large piece off someone else's timber? You must also consider the practical side of obtaining a saw stout enough to cut through such a branch. Do you have the strength to do this? How are you going to get it home once it is cut? Do you have a place at home where you can store it unobtrusively?

These may all seem like non-magical things to think about, but any magical Work should follow normal guidelines of practicality and manageability. This is what separates the Working, achieving magician from the airy-fairy, would-be magician who cannot live successfully in this world, never mind operating in the Otherworld.

When you have solved all these problems, answered all these questions, and finally taken your ash branch home, you can set about creating your Spear. Completely strip the bark, and give the branch long enough to dry thoroughly before you do anything else. Removing the bark will be a time-consuming process, during which you should be focusing on what the Spear represents, who Lugh is, and what he means to you and to the Spear you are fashioning, what you want the finished Weapon to look like, and when you may want to use it.

The next stage is to carefully smooth out any bumps, rough patches, or stumps of smaller branches that make the Spear rough and uneven. Polish the length of it with sand paper and give it as smooth and even a finish as you can. Next, fashion the tip of the Spear by carving a long, hard point, or purchase an antique spear head from a military dealer or antique shop. Carve or decorate the shaft of the Spear with meaningful symbols, colors, or designs, if you like. This is your personal tool, and how it looks and feels is entirely your decision. Once the process is complete, you must dedicate this new Magical Weapon. Like all of your Magical Weapons, it should be stored in a special place and not be used for mundane tasks or to shown off to friends or relatives.

The ceremonial uses of the Spear are twofold: It is the larger version of the Wand, to be used during group rituals. Its second use is on a personal level, when the work you are undertaking is of a higher, more powerful nature, or when you are going through a period of inertia and stagnation. Whenever or however you use it, you should always call upon Lugh for guidance and assistance.

Once you feel you have succeeded in your communications with the ash, try the following exercise: Take your five Ogham sticks into your magical Working area. This time do not draw the circle around a particular tree, but instead draw it around yourself. Lay out your Ogham sticks in the order given in this book, and see how one has developed from the other. Then, spend some time arranging them in different orders. Think over what you have learned from your study of these five trees, and try to build a picture of how they relate to each other.

When you have a feel for the way the trees link one with the other in shifting and changing ways, close your eyes, call upon the Daghdha for guidance, and start an Otherworld journey. Let the imagery flow freely, and do not try to predict what is going to happen. I would suggest you start by visualizing yourself standing in a forest with the five trees as the predominant species. See the Ogham letter for each one carved on its trunk. Start to walk as you note carefully the order in which you pass these trees. Think on how you feel, and how much you remember about each of the trees. Try to notice if the trees change, depending upon which other tree or trees they are near. Watch for any animals, birds, or people who may appear during this journey; they, too, may have much to tell you. Take note of any species that may be more plentiful than others, or which may appeal to you more than the rest. This could be an indication of an aspect of your life or Work that needs special attention.

When you are familiar with this landscape, call upon your Otherworld guide to make him or herself known to you. This may take several repetitive journeys to achieve, but stick with it until you have established a conscious link. By doing this, you will eventually build a coherent and very meaningful relationship with this nonphysical being. You will find that contact becomes stronger the more you wade through the trees. Don't worry if it doesn't go well at first; there will be many more opportunities to achieve this contact.

As always on closing, record as much detail as you can in your magical diary, even if little or nothing seemed to happen. Repeat this exercise until you feel you are starting to make your own links and connections between yourself, the trees, and your Otherworld guide. Once you are satisfied, proceed to the next tree in the sequence.

CHAPTER TEN

HAWTHORN

Name: Huath
Letter: H
Ogham letter: ⊥
Textual reference: Huath is Whitethorn, a meet of hounds is Whitethorn, it is formidable owing to its thorns.
Word Ogham of Morainn: CONDAL CON, pack of wolves.
Word Ogham of Cuchulain: ANNSAM AIDHCHE .i. HUATH, difficult night, Hawthorn.
Word Ogham of Aonghus: BANAD GNUISI, whitening of face.

Physical Level

The hawthorn, whitethorn, or quickthorn can grow to a height of forty-five feet. These days, it is usually cut back to form low, thick hedges, and is rarely seen as a full-grown tree. It is very distinctive, with its profusion of small, white flowers in May, which turn to bright red berries and darker, fleshy fruits, known as haws, later in the year. Its bark is grayish-brown, flecked with small scales, and covered with the very hard and sharp thorns that give the tree its name. Its leaves, which are on alternate sides of the prickly, twisted stalks, have deeply divided lobes, giving them a similar appearance to small oak leaves. The leaves make a pleasant tea good for people with cardiac or circulatory problems. It is also a remedy for those

109

suffering from sudden emotional distress, or for people with long-term nervous conditions. The juice can also be used in the treatment of asthma, rheumatism, arthritis, and laryngitis.

The wood of the hawthorn is rarely used commercially, as its branches are very knotted and not of much use to the carver or woodworker. It does not burn well either, and has long been the subject of superstition that says that it is unlucky to bring hawthorn into the house. It is often found growing on fairy hills, the Sidhe mounds described in the legends. It is commonly believed to have been placed there by the fairies as a warning to humans, in order to protect the mound, for no sensible person would ever disturb such a tree. When the DeLorean car company opened its factory in Ireland, part of the development site included such a mound, with a hawthorn growing from it. None of the Irish workmen would remove the mound and, eventually, John DeLorean himself drove the bulldozer to clear it away. History has shown the grave error of his actions.

Hawthorn is most often found today forming hedges along country lanes, where its closely-knitted branches and sharp thorns make it ideal for the purpose. When it is allowed to grow wild, it can take on some very peculiar shapes, and is often found standing alone in the middle of a field or hillside. Perhaps it was this unusual characteristic that encouraged the belief that it had been planted by fairies. Despite its gnarled appearance and formidable thorns, the hawthorn in full bloom is a very attractive tree. Many old folksongs mention hawthorn in one context or another, and the surname, Hawthorn, is still quite common among English-speaking people.

Mental Level

The word for this tree, *Huath*, or *Uath*, means "frightful" or "horrible," and provides a clue to its magical virtues and uses. The description in the textual references, "a meet of hounds," and in the Word Oghams of Morainn, Cuchulain, and Aonghus, "pack of wolves, difficult night, whitening of face," also suggest this unpleasant aspect.

All the trees we have examined so far can be used consciously and deliberately as an integral part of an Otherworld journey, to initiate new Work appropriate to the meanings and virtues of each tree. Hawthorn, however, is very different, and has a very different function. We began to examine this in our discussion of the Ogham Alphabet in Part One. The letter H has a distinct function within the rules of Gaelic grammar as neither consonant nor vowel. Similarly, the Hawthorn has a distinct function within the normal rules of tree magic, and should not be used by the magician as a deliberate symbol invoked during Otherworld journeys or rituals. Its magical function is as a symbol to be used only by those in the Otherworld as a warning to the magician to prepare for something about to happen. It should arise spontaneously and, I hope, infrequently during Workings. It should never be sought out by the Otherworld traveler. If it does arise, it usually indicates that something you started, perhaps at another level, is taking effect, and the inevitable backlash is about to hit you. This is not as ominous as it seems, although the backlash can be quite unpleasant. If it is expected and understood for what it is, then most of the sting is taken out of it, and it will be easier to cope with.

This is a rule of magic that magicians—experienced and inexperienced—must understand. If you start any magical Working that uses new energies, or sets up a new chain of events, there is always a backlash. It may be as simple as your feeling out of sorts for a few days. The Word Ogham of Aonghus refers to this as the "whitening of face." It may manifest as a feeling of irritability, which causes arguments between people who normally get along well together. This is what Morainn's "pack of wolves" reference warns. It may even manifest as a deep-rooted fear, tension, or depression. This is the "difficult night" in the Word Ogham of Cuchulain.

The hawthorn is used by the Otherworld to show you that the unpleasantness of the backlash is temporary, and is nothing to worry about. Although this experience can be difficult, especially for the less-experienced magician, it should be seen as positive and encouraging, indicating to you that your early magical actions have been successful. Often when this first occurs to the fledgling magician, he or she starts to imagine some sort of psychic attack from anonymous black magicians who are trying to disrupt the Work at hand. This is rarely the case, and any such notions can be replaced with the positive knowledge that, despite immediate feelings and concerns, things are going very well.

The hawthorn is often regarded as hostile and offensive because of its sharp thorns and tangled branches, but these same thorns and branches can be defensive and protective, keeping at bay that which is trying to hurt you. This is another level of meaning for "meet of hounds" and "pack of wolves." In old Irish, these are puns playing on the word *cu* ("dog" or "wolf"), which also means "warrior." Meet of hounds and pack of wolves can be translated as meet of warriors and pack of warriors. A pack of warriors standing back to back, with their ash spears bristling outwards, is just like a hawthorn bush with its sharp thorns sticking out, ready to repel any who come too close. It is a very protective tree, suggestive of a brief period of difficulty; but, ultimately, it is a tree of good omen and hope.

The hawthorn was used by groups within ancient Celtic society on a physical level as well as on the mental and spiritual levels. When it was used physically, it was a malicious and hostile symbol, associated with the practice of satire (the composition of verse describing an individual's bad points). This seemingly quaint means of attack was considered a terrifying thing to the Celts; to have a satire made against you was the worst thing that could possibly happen. In his three-volume set, *Manners and Customs of the Ancient Irish*, Eugene O'Curry quotes a strange practice employed by the satirists which reads:

The face of the Ollamh towards the land of the king whom he would satirize, and the backs of them all towards a hawthorn...and a slingstone and a thorn of the hawthorn in every man's hand and each of them to sing a stave in a prescribed metre into the slingstone and the thorn...and each was then to put his stone and his thorn at the foot of the hawthorn.[1]

This shows how trees were used on the physical level as magical weapons, just as they were used in the Otherworld as magical symbols. This is the three levels working in harmony, the physical level just as useful and powerful as the other two. It is also one of the warnings of the hawthorn—to confine your magical Work to only the mental and spiritual levels is foolish.

A satire against a person in the form of libel or slander can be a totally destructive thing, even if it is untrue. The power to damage a person by words alone is tremendous, and is a power which you would best leave alone. The ancient Celts knew this, and it was only after many years of arduous training that one was given the title of Bard and permitted to satirize others.

Spiritual Level

The power of H is that it increases the power of other letters in a grammatical context. This applies equally to the power of hawthorn on a spiritual level. Once the magical or spiritual Work is finished, you must expect a period of disruption, which should not be too severe or upsetting. This negative period can be put to positive use as a time for you to recharge your spiritual batteries by contemplating the success of the magical or spiritual operation that is causing the upset. This may seem contradictory, but you must remember that

[1] Eugene O'Curry, *Manners and Customs of the Ancient Irish.*

energy is neutral, and only appears negative or positive depending upon your reaction to it. This reflection on your success is not to be an unhealthy wallowing in self praise, or the start of an uncontrollable ego; it is a well-deserved and quite acceptable recognition of your abilities and skills. Acknowledging these has the effect of strengthening them for the next time you call upon them. Use hawthorn to increase and improve your spiritual aspirations through understanding the reason behind your suffering, and by turning the whole experience into a positive and useful one. The Ogham notch for the hawthorn is the first to stand upright, proud and straight. Be like that notch as you go about your business.

Hawthorn offers rest and recuperation before the next new piece of Work is tackled. Before moving on, remember to carry out your tree ritual, and take note of any realizations or communications you have. These may not be pleasant, but they must be faced and experienced, and you must learn from them.

Practical Work

Because the hawthorn symbolizes something outside the normal rule of things, this is a good time for you to introduce into your Practical Work something new, personal, and innovative. This may be a new set of movements or words connected with the ritual, or it could be a total change in the time and way in which you go about these practical exercises. It may be a spontaneous Otherworld journey, or series of journeys, designed to help you cope with fear, trepidation, and other difficult emotions the hawthorn will throw at you. Your Work will become more special, powerful, and meaningful to you. The onus of your progress will begin to lay fairly and squarely on your shoulders. Are you going to take this responsibility and devise your own private aspect to these Workings? Are you going to accept the responsibility of bearing the great weight of your own spiritual progress? Think about this. Keep in mind that, according to this ancient magical system, anything you do—good or bad, successful or unsuccessful—on the physical level will be reflected on your spiritual level. The Daghdha and your personal guide should be able to help you. You also have the knowledge and experience of the previous five trees to fall back on when things get too confusing.

This would be a good time to enter into a serious dialogue with your guide in an attempt to come up with some Practical Work that will provide answers to questions you may have, or which will help to provide solutions for problems you may face in your day-to-day life. This is what your guide and practical magic are all about.

CHAPTER ELEVEN

OAK

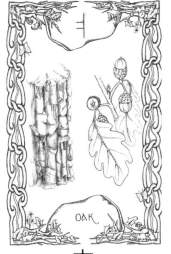

Name: Duir
Letter: D
Ogham letter: ⊥⊥
Textual reference: Duir, Oak, higher than bushes is an Oak.
Word Ogham of Morainn: ARDDAM DOSSA, highest of bushes and TRIAN a third.
Word Ogham of Cuchulain: SLECHTAIN SAIRE .i. NIAMA SAIRTE, kneeling work, bright and shining work.
Word Ogham of Aonghus: GRES SAIR, craft work.

Physical Level

The oak is the tree most associated with the druids, and is a very important tree. Its short trunk, supporting a large, full crown growing to as much as one-hundred-fifteen feet, is a truly splendid sight. Its bark is at first smooth, shiny, and light gray in color but, as the tree ages, the bark starts to crack, and fissures appear around the trunk. Its leaves are on alternate sides of the stalks and are lobed, usually with four or five lobes on each side, giving them a very distinctive shape. The fruit of the oak takes the form of acorns, an important foodstuff to both wild and domestic animals. The oak bears small, female flowers in May, when the leaves appear, as well as the long, slim, yellow male catkins.

The wood of the oak is hard and was nearly the cause of its extinction in Britain, when vast forests of oak were cut to provide timber for ships for the Elizabethan navy. The trees were also felled in great numbers to provide high-quality charcoal for smiths' forges. Eventually, laws were passed to afford the tree some protection and give it time to reestablish itself in what must have been the earliest recorded attempt at ecological preservation through legislation.

The oak's bark provides tannin, which was used extensively in the leather industry for tanning raw hides. The younger, lighter-grained branches are still much in demand today for furniture manufacturing. It is one of the longest lived trees, taking seventy to eighty years before producing acorns. It is home to a large variety of bird, animal, and insect life, with up to a hundred species of insects competing for space within its bark. This, in itself, shows what a hardy tree it is.

Acorns can be used to make a very powerful antiseptic, and the juice from crushed oak leaves can be applied directly to wounds for the same purpose. A gargle made from the inner bark is useful to relieve sore throats and catarrh, and a decoction of the outer bark can help relieve severe fever symptoms. The leaves, if soaked in boiling water and allowed to cool, can be a very soothing potion for tired or inflamed eyes. A decoction of acorns and bark is supposed to be a good antidote for poison, and also helps women experiencing pain or discomfort during their menstrual cycles.

The Irish surname MacDara means "son of the oak." Place names such as Derry and Kildare are derived from the old name for the oak. It is often argued by Celtic scholars that the root of the word druid lies in an old word for oak.

Mental Level

The oak is already popularly associated with druids, magic, and the king of the trees. All of these associations are useful and can be employed by the magician. The name given in the Word Ogham of

Morainn, *Arddam Dossa*, is usually translated as "highest or most exalted of bushes." There is a deliberate pun in this expression, for *Dossa* can also mean "sheltering defense" or "protecting chief." The oak can be considered the highest of defenses, or even the most exalted of chiefs who offers protection. Any ancient warrior, whether of this world or the Otherworld, at some point in his or her soldierings would have needed both the shelter and protection of a chief or king. The same applies to the modern-day warriors in the guise of magicians. You may be able to go it alone for a while, but inevitably you will need rest and protection as can only be provided by a higher authority or, symbolically, a king. This respite can be found in the shady branches of the majestic oak tree. In a passage from the *Lays of Fionn*, there is a section where Fionn is planning to slay his archenemy Goll mac Morna. Fionn eventually finds Goll:

> A spell of sleep was taken thereafter by Morna's son so
> that Fionn heard the groaning breath of the hero hard by
> the oak.[1]

Note that the oak is identified as the tree underneath which Goll chose to take his rest. As legend relates, Fionn did not attack him, and he escaped unscathed, clearly indicating the oak's sheltering and protective qualities. This protective quality is further emphasized in a text known as *Lebor Na Cert (Book of Rights)*, which is a great list of payments and stipends due to certain personages throughout Ireland.

> Fifty horns and fifty swords, fifty properly harnessed
> horses to the prosperous man from the oak-groves of the
> goodly mast, to the prince of Ailech who protects all.[2]

---

[1] Gerard Murphy, trans., *Duanaire Finn* (Dublin: Irish Texts Society, 1933).
[2] Myles Dillon, trans., *Lebor na Cert* (Dublin: Irish Texts Society, 1962).

A poem from the same source contains a verse which says:

> My rank and my lordship
>
> my beauty and my fame
>
> my nobility and my endurance
>
> my cherished ancestral possessions
>
> my power and my protection
>
> to my chosen champion Rus,
>
> to my noble Failge of the red blade
>
> to my strong and sturdy shelter of good oak.[3]

The oak is strongly connected with the institution of king, and especially the High King, with his spiritual link to the land. The warrior connection is also brought into play in a passage from the "Cattle Raid of Cooley," in which the great Ulster hero, Cuchulain, is being pursued by the armies of Queen Meadhbh of Connacht. At a place called Mag Muicceda, Cuchulain cut down an oak tree with a single blow of his sword, and stuck it in the middle of the road along which Meadhbh's warriors would come. He inscribed upon it a message in Ogham, forbidding any to pass until a warrior had leaped the oak in his chariot. Thirty warriors tried and failed. Later, Fraoch fought with Cuchulain and was killed by him and, immediately after, Fearghus managed to leap the oak and allow the army to move on. Although no more is said in this passage about the Ogham itself, it was clearly of some powerful magical significance. More will be said of Fraoch when we examine the heather.

The word for oak used in the *Beithe Luis Nion, Duir,* is sometimes given as *dair,* common in Ireland in names such as Derry and Kildare, both of which were huge oak groves used by the Celts as

---

[3] Ibid.

sacred sites. The word, *dair,* also has a second meaning that describes a rutting deer. Once again, there is a connection between deer and kingship. To the Celts, the noble stag was the king of the beasts. A rutting stag was likely to turn on its attacker rather than run away, as deer usually do; therefore, he was treated with respect and caution. This association between the oak and the stag is shown in another passage from the *Lays of Fionn* that says:

> It was the glorious hunting which gave the Cooking
> Copse its name: a hundred stags from every oak-grove
> that held a bush we laid low around Ruadhros.[4]

The various meanings for the oak provide symbolism for use in Otherworld journeys and rituals, if fully understood and carefully thought out beforehand. The use of an oak grove during an Otherworld journey can be very powerful. Important events tend to occur once you find yourself within such a grove. You cannot force significant happenings merely by imagining yourself within an oak grove; however, should you stumble across such a place during your Otherworld rambling, you should take careful note of the events that follow. Similarly, the appearance of a rutting stag can be of great significance, and should be noted and treated with caution both in your actions and thoughts. How you react to these things can greatly influence their outcome.

Spiritual Level

The oak, on the spiritual level, symbolizes the successful completion of your personal progress through the other trees that make up the Tree Ogham. By the time you reach the oak grove, the dreadful events of the hawthorn are behind you. You have completed the magical Work that resulted in the hawthorn experiences, and have

---

[4] Murphy, *Duanaire Finn.*

the added bonus of having learned from those experiences. Now is the time to Work under the protection of the highest of bushes, the most exalted king, who offers protection as you set off once again on your road to progress and discovery. This is nicely symbolized by the Ogham notch for oak, which is two uprights next to each other—you, and your protecting High King.

At this level, one deity you can consider to be your protecting king is the Daghdha, the good god. Of all the trees, the oak is most closely connected with the Daghdha. This is demonstrated in a passage from the "Battle of Moytura," where a girl from the Otherworld is trying to prevent the Daghdha from traveling his rightful course.

> "You will not go past me until I summon the sons of Tethra from the sid-mounds, because I will be a giant oak in every ford and in every pass you will cross."
>
> "I will indeed go past," said the Daghdha, "and the mark of my axe will remain in every oak forever." And people have remarked upon the mark of the Daghdha's axe.[5]

The Daghdha is the archetypal figure when Working with oak on a spiritual level. He is also associated with rutting deer, and is closely linked with the earth and the physical level, emphasized in the many legends about him. The legends graphically detail his great appetite for food and sex, his crude appearance, and his ability to pass huge amounts of bodily waste. They also illustrate his close association with the Cauldron of Plenty and the sharing of food, hospitality, and protection. People coming new to this system are often surprised or confused by this emphasis on physical things, when we seemingly should be dealing with spiritual matters. In order to experience one level fully, however, you must experience

---

[5] E.A. Gray, trans., *Cath Maige Tuired*, (Dublin: Irish Texts Society, 1983).

the other. In practical terms, you must become deeply involved in the mundane events of your life. You must examine your own sexual desires and impulses, your own bodily functions, abilities, and constitution. The Daghdha will make this clear to you as he helps you appreciate the spiritual level of the oak tree. Because of our upbringing, most of us will have at least some difficulty managing this, with a whole lifetime of conditioning to fight.

The Daghdha's other great attribute is his generous hospitality and willingness to share the good things of this life, as symbolized by his ever-full cauldron. This is another part of High Kingship that must become a part of your day-to-day life. You will have to answer honestly questions such as, just how generous are you? How willing are you to share what you have with total strangers, or maybe even people you don't like? Are you still clinging to physical possessions, bad mental habits, or incorrect spiritual leanings, simply because you cannot bring yourself to get rid of them? You must deal with all of these things to progress through the spiritual level of the oak; however, the reward for those who complete this test will be to sit at the cauldron of the Daghdha, and share what he has to offer. You cannot cheat. The cauldron will appear empty to cowards and liars, and full only to those who have learned to face their true selves.

The connection between the physical, spiritual, and your Work is suggested in the Word Oghams of Aonghus and Cuchulain as "craft work" and "kneeling work" that is "bright and shining work." It is vital that you keep yourself securely anchored in this world, and do not drift into some fantasy world, away with the fairies. The word for work, *saire*, also means "freedom." If you read the above comments, substituting freedom for work, even more of the oak's spiritual secrets will be revealed.

Once through the whole experience of the oak, you will become your own High King, and be in a position to pass on your knowledge and experiences to those who come to you for shelter. While this may seem beyond what you hope to achieve, remember that the function of the High King is purely a spiritual one. When you recognize and accept your spiritual self and worth, you will have attained a state of High Kingship for which you can feel proud and satisfied.

Practical Work

There is a lot to be learned from the oak tree. You may find that you spend longer with the oak than with any of the other trees so far. Pay particular attention to the Daghdha during your ritual with the oak. Although he has been present with every tree, the oak is his personal tree, and he can shed a lot of light on its magical and spiritual aspects.

Now is the time to be on the lookout for a Cauldron. The Cauldron is the Greater version of your magical Cup. The Daghdha is associated with the magical Cauldron of Murias, the nature of which was that it would feed all who came to it with whatever they desired, but that cowards and liars would find it empty. Like the other Greater Magical Weapons, its uses are in ceremonial group Work, as a substitute for your personal Cup, and in solitary Work that requires greater energy.

Not many people use cauldrons as a household item today, however some occult suppliers stock Cauldrons for magical use. If you have the skills, you may be able to fashion your own Cauldron, which would make it especially meaningful to you. When you set your mind to obtaining a Cauldron, you will find that it comes to you when you are ready. The test will be whether you are considered a coward or a liar by those in the Otherworld who are watching your progress through the Ogham forest. None of these Magical Weapons are given freely, or without conditions. You must be pure in body, heart, and spirit to earn what is rightfully yours. These are the same conditions of eligibility for High Kingship.

By now, you may be developing a concept of the whole of this system. All of the concepts we've discussed are beginning to come together for you. This is the time to consider your own High

Kingship, your spiritual link with the land and the trees. In ancient Ireland, the test of eligibility for High Kingship was to stand on the Lia Fail, the Stone of Destiny, which would cry aloud when the true High King placed his foot upon it.

Incorporate this idea into your next ritual by taking a large, flat stone into your Working Area with you. Once you have begun to make contact with the oak, let go of your Ogham stick and stand on the stone. Close your eyes and imagine the flow of energy coming from deep within the earth, flowing up through your feet, legs, spine, and eventually to the inside of your cranium, where it turns and flows back into the earth to form a complete circuit. You have now made a very real link with the earth energies and, in so doing, have taken on the duties of the High King. These duties may include protecting those who come to you for help. Think carefully on this. Are you ready? Consider the Daghdha, too, when you mull over these points. This is exactly what he is doing—accepting without question or discrimination all who come to him for guidance and protection. He should be able to give you some good advice on what this really means, and how to achieve it. Listen, also, to any words your guide has to say on this subject.

CHAPTER TWELVE

HOLLY

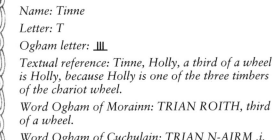

Name: Tinne

Letter: T

Ogham letter: ᚈ

Textual reference: Tinne, Holly, a third of a wheel is Holly, because Holly is one of the three timbers of the chariot wheel.

Word Ogham of Morainn: TRIAN ROITH, third of a wheel.

Word Ogham of Cuchulain: TRIAN N-AIRM .i. TINNE IAIRM, a third of weapons, an iron bar.

Word Ogham of Aonghus: SMIUR GUAILE, fires of coal.

Physical Level

Holly trees are rarely allowed to grow to their full height of sixty-five feet and are instead trimmed down as hedges or ornamental bushes. This tree is probably one most people can identify with confidence, with its evergreen leaves and bright red berries. Its sharp, prickly leaves are shiny and waxy and grow on alternate sides of the tough stalks. The male and female trees both bear small, lightly scented flowers, but it is only the female tree that bears the distinctive red berries. Its bark starts out smooth and green, but grows gray and rougher as the tree ages. The wood is white, sometimes with a greenish tinge to it, and is very hard and heavy. It is ideally suited to carving and for use as an inlay for marquetry and furniture making.

Tea made from the leaves of the holly is a very stimulating and invigorating drink, and will induce sweating to help rid the body of accumulated poisons and lingering fevers. If eaten when ripe, its berries act as a strong purgative, excellent at clearing the body of unwanted waste material. If dried and powdered before consuming, they have the opposite effect of relieving diarrhea and heavy menstrual flows. The bark and leaves can be made into poultices that are excellent for placing on broken and setting bones.

The holly is closely associated with winter and Christmas due to its evergreen properties, which make it ideal for decorative wreaths. The word holly appears in many place names throughout the English-speaking world, and it is a common surname and girl's forename.

Mental Level

As we learned during our examination of the letters of the *Beithe Luis Nion* in Chapter Three, the letter T is really another form of the letter D. The holly tree, too, can be considered to be another form of the oak, at least on a magical level. This is implied in the Word Ogham of Morainn where the oak, *Arddam Dossa*, "highest of bushes and *Trian* a third," includes the word *Trian*, which is a name for holly. Its own Word Ogham references seem to downplay the holly's importance even more, stating that it is a mere third of the wood used in the construction of chariot wheels, or a third of weapons. The word *trian* means "third." Note that the Ogham notch for this tree consists of three uprights.

A passage from the "Cattle Raid of Cooley" deals with the repair of chariots, and states that chariots were made with shafts of holly as opposed to any other wood. We also learn from this legend that holly was used as a weapon. Two separate passages make reference to this. In one, we are told that the warrior Nadcranntail went into battle, taking with him nine spears of holly, charred and sharpened (note the reference to the magical number nine). The other says that during battle, a piece of split holly drove into Cuchulain's foot, and its point came out at his knee, and he flung his holly spear after Ferbaeth.

The wheel of the chariot lifts the body of the chariot off the ground and allows it to progress. A weapon is the instrument needed to clear unwanted or hostile adversaries out of the way. We need to do both of these things today: progress and remove obstacles in our path; therefore, these two ancient symbols are still valid and useful in the Tree Ogham system of practical magic and spiritual progress. The constant reference to a third is also important, as the number three was of very special significance to the ancient Celts. It is the number of levels of existence, and it is the way everything manifests in this world, with a left half, a right half, and a part that is in between the two. The third referred to in the text is the in-between third, the very magical one.

Holly is a substitute for the noble oak and is an important tree in its own right, despite the apparent attempts to gloss over it in the Word Oghams. From a magical point of view, it is preferable to Work with the holly as a substitute for oak when initially attempting magical Work on the trees. This has the effect of making the powers of the oak even stronger and more important when you eventually progress to Working directly with that tree.

The *Tainaiste,* in magical Working, is that part of your being that, somewhere along the line, may be asked to lay down its life as a substitute for the oak king. This does not mean that you will be expected to give up your life in this world to complete some magical Working, but it does mean that you may be expected to sacrifice something in order to progress. This is a perfectly acceptable circumstance, and something which actually happens all the time in your day-to-day life. Your magical life should be an extension of your mundane life. If you have progressed through the various trees and reached the oak level successfully, then understanding this principle will not be hard for you.

The relationship between the oak and the holly is a complex one that everybody interprets in their own way. To understand the double aspect of the oak and holly, you must Work with both of these trees on all levels until you have formed your own opinions of how they fit into your magical and daily lives. Once you have achieved this, you will have created the *trian* aspect—the third aspect—the trinity of oak, holly, and Self.

Spiritual Level

The holly is a symbolic tree that will prove to be very powerful on the spiritual level as you get to know it. Its symbolism lies in the fact that it is an evergreen, which demonstrates its ability to live and bloom despite harsh climatic changes and the turning of the seasons. It is a powerful symbol of the continuation of life after physical death, and of reincarnation to the physical level.[1] To gain a deep spiritual understanding of these principles shows true progress. You will have realized the often forgotten point that the oak, the king of the trees, is not the end in itself. There is yet a greater power behind the High King.

The name for holly in the Tree Ogham, *Tinne*, can mean "link," as in a chain. This is a valuable symbol of the holly's link with the oak, its link between this world and the Otherworld, and the link joining the three levels. Deep, spiritual meditation on these points will prove enlightening. The holly's position in the Tree Ogham

---

[1] While the belief in reincarnation is important to this system of magic, it is no more important than any other aspect. I would advise you not to spend a disproportionate amount of time considering the viability of this doctrine. Think about it, come to your own understanding of what it means and how it works, but do not give it excessive attention relative to the other points raised.

sequence is exactly halfway through the fifteen consonants. It is the pivotal point around which all the other letters revolve. This, too, can be viewed symbolically as the point between life and death, or death and rebirth. It is the point where one changes to the other, where we begin to return to the beginning.

The next tree in the sequence will teach us how to progress further along what has now become a circle of knowledge and experience. You may find that your Practical Work takes on a new vitality, or a shift in awareness. Don't neglect this important Practical Work. Take your time with it, and record faithfully all that comes to you.

Practical Work

Carry out the tree ritual until you are familiar with the holly. Then, because of holly's unique relationship with oak, try the basic Working with holly and oak. Understanding this relationship is important to grasping the deeper principles behind the Celtic system. Alternate sessions using your holly Ogham stick to connect with the oak, and then using your oak Ogham stick to connect with the holly. Take careful note of how this new technique feels. Be aware of the subtle differences between connecting with the oak and connecting with the holly in this way.

You may feel some disorientation during the weeks you are linking with the holly. This is nothing to be concerned about. You are placing yourself in an in-between state of awareness of two things at once. This is not the way we normally function, but it is the way we must learn to function to gain the ability to move between the physical world and the Otherworld. Your guide will help you here; this is one of his or her main functions.

It has now become particularly important to ensure that you close each ritual fully, and that you take a few moments to adjust to your "normal" way of thinking. You are starting to get into deeper realms of Celtic tree magic, and a firm grounding in the physical will help tremendously. The more you perform your basic ritual, the more powerful it becomes. The more you link with the Daghdha, the stronger that link becomes. The more you listen to your Otherworld guide, and take his or her advice, the more powerful that link becomes, too. In short, the more you do these exercises, the more powerful you become. Power brings responsibility. Be sure you are ready and willing to accept this responsibility before progressing further.

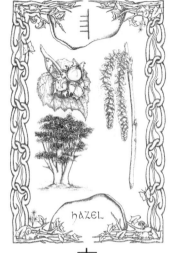

CHAPTER THIRTEEN

HAZEL

Name: Coll

Letter: C

Ogham letter: ⚞

Textual reference: Coll, fair wood that is Hazel everyone is eating of its nuts.

Word Ogham of Morainn: CAINIU FEDAIR, fairest of trees.

Word Ogham of Cuchulain: MILLSEM FEDHO .i. CNO, sweetest of woods, a nut.

Word Ogham of Aonghus: CARA BLOISC, friend of cracking.

Physical Level

The hazel is not a particularly large tree, reaching only thirty feet in height if allowed to grow unmolested. It is often cut back and coppiced, like the willow, to produce long, straight rods that are used for many of the same things as willow rods. The bark of the tree is scaly, light brown, and often with yellowish pores. The leaves are on alternate sides of the stalk, ragged at the edges, hairy, and up to four inches across. In February, the tree takes on a strong yellow hue, when it is covered with long, male catkins and tiny female flowers with their red-tufted leaves covering the hazelnuts, which grow in small clusters of three or four.

The nuts of the hazel are rich in mineral salts, and perfectly palatable just as they are. They can be ground into a powder that when mixed with a drink, is good for soothing a sore throat and relieving the symptoms of a head cold. The dry husks, shells, and red skin covering the nut itself can similarly be powdered to drink for the relief of unusually heavy menstrual flows. The wood is used for many of the same purposes as willow, and is cultivated and harvested in the same manner. The pliant twigs of the hazel are a favorite for dowsers, who use a fork-shaped branch in the dowsing of water and other minerals and elements.

The hazel has been well established in the British Isles and Ireland for a very long time, as proven by examination of pollen deposits taken from archaeological sites throughout the islands. Deposits show that the trees were planted and managed by the locals ages ago, presumably because of the many uses of the tree for food and medicine.

The name Hazel has long been a favorite for girls, and the surname MacCuill, or more commonly MacColl and MacCall, means "son of the hazel." The common Scottish place name, Calton or Carlton, is a corruption of the old Gaelic name for the tree, and indicates a place—often a hill—where a substantial number of hazel trees would have grown, perhaps in the form of a sacred grove. The persistence of the name long after the trees have gone shows the great importance these trees have under this system.

Mental Level

The description in the Word Ogham of Morainn, "fairest of trees," is rather odd, as the hazel appears no fairer than any other tree. We should therefore consider this a hint to look for a deeper meaning in this misleading title. The name "fairest of trees" is given in Irish as *Cainiu Fedaib.* The deeper meaning of this expression lies in the alternative meanings of *cainiu,* "to keen over a death" or "to satirize someone." The origin of keening, weeping, and wailing is attributed the goddess Brighid, following the death of her son Ruadhan during the Battle of Moytura. The modern Gaelic name for the tree is *Calltuinn,* a word that means "the loss of something," and which can clearly be connected to death and, therefore, to keening.

The hazel is connected with death and keening in another way in that one of the versions of the death of Balor, the evil king of the Fomhoire, says that after Lugh cut off his hideous head, he placed it in the fork of a hazel tree. Evil poison dripped out of the severed neck and fell upon the hazel. A poem from the *Lays of Fionn* says that the hazel remained in this poisonous state for fifty years, until Manannan, the sea god, felled it. Later, Fionn used the wood to make a shield he called Dripping Ancient Hazel. Fionn's own surname is variously given as Mac Cuill or Mac Coll, both of which mean "Son of the Hazel."

Brighid is the goddess most closely associated with wisdom and divine inspiration, and herein lies the deeper meaning of the hazel. There are several legends centering on magic hazel trees whose nuts contained all wisdom. The practice of satirizing is also closely linked to divine inspiration and poetry. The original satirists were poets whose matron was Brighid. Satire was considered to be so powerful and potentially destructive that only certain grades of bards or druids were allowed to perform it. There were very strict laws governing how it should be done, when it should be used, and what the penalties were for its improper use. Druids, when performing the elaborate ritual known as *Dichetel Do Chenaid,* are said to have chewed hazelnuts as a means of attaining inspiration and knowledge of something hidden or lost. Hazel was also used to focus the mind prior to uttering a devastating satire.

The use of hazel trees and, particularly, hazelnuts is recommended during Otherworld journeys and rituals where the purpose is to gain knowledge. Heralds are the bearers of knowledge, and a passage from the "Cattle Raid of Cooley" describes a herald as

A dark, handsome man with a broad face. He had a brown brooch in his splendid brown cloak with a strong shirt next his skin. Between his feet and the ground were his worn shoes. He held a peeled hazel wand in one hand and a single-edged sword with guards of ivory in the other.[1]

A wand of hazel was a recognized symbol for a herald, and is a good symbol to look out for during Otherworld journeys. Consider, too, that it is hazel branches that are most favored by dowsers for locating hidden streams and buried metals. The fact that it takes nine years for the hazel to bear fruit is a further suggestion of its magical connections on the physical level.

Three of the earliest kings of Ireland were brothers called Mac Ceacht, Mac Greine, and Mac Coll. These names mean "Son of the Plough," "Son of the Sun," and "Son of the Hazel." This creates a link with the hazel to the High King and to the fertility of the land.

Spiritual Level

The presence of the hazel shows you that you still have much to learn from trees and the Tree Ogham. The deity most closely associated with the hazel is Brighid, and consciously Working with her at a spiritual level, in conjunction with the hazel, should prove very illuminating on all levels. There are many legends involving Brighid, and these should give you ideas and symbols to make conscious contact with her easier.[2] Besides being the pre-Christian goddess of the Tuatha De Danann, there is also the later Christian St. Brighid, who probably owes her existence to the early pagan goddess. If you

---

[1] Cecile O'Rahilly, *Tain Bo Cuailgne* (Dublin: Irish Texts Society, 1962).
[2] I devoted a whole section of my earlier book, *Glamoury: Magic of the Celtic Green World*, to Brighid and her festival of Imbolg. The Bibliography at the end of this book will guide the newcomer to sources of legends, symbols, and characters to be used during Otherworld journeys.

feel more comfortable Working with the image of the saint than the image of the ancient goddess, it is perfectly acceptable to do so. Always remember that, during Otherworld journeys, it is what these non-human guides say and do that is important, and not who they claim to be. Studying the lives of saints can be just as useful to tree magic as is the study of the more obvious connection with pre-Christian mythology. The early Christian monks who wrote about the lives of the saints were the same people who wrote the *Book of Ballymote,* the *Book of Leinster,* and the other manuscripts that give us so much valuable knowledge about Ogham and tree magic.

The process of making conscious contact with Brighid is one that needs to be repeated. Just as the hazel brings forth new nuts each year, so, too, are there new things to be learned and experienced throughout the whole of life. The partaking of the hazelnuts of wisdom should be an ongoing affair, and not something that is done once and then forgotten. The Word Ogham of Aonghus, "friend of cracking," refers to the cracking open of the hazelnuts of wisdom. This is probably why the Word Ogham of Cuchulain refers to it as "sweetest of woods, a nut."

Practical Work

The hazel is a tree you will need to return to again and again in your Practical Work to get the most from it. It is also the first tree where the fruit plays an important role in its own right. You can incorporate this into your basic ritual by eating hazelnuts, when they are in season, as you link with the hazel tree. You can, of course, eat hazelnuts any time, and use this as a mnemonic aid for recalling what the hazel means to you. The nuts of the hazel, according to legend, contain all wisdom. Be aware of this as you do the Practical Work for this tree.

You should also develop a relationship with Brighid, as she will have much to tell you. According to some genealogies, Brighid is the daughter of the Daghdha. This family link between the two deities associated with the hazel can be put to good advantage in obtaining knowledge from father and daughter.

Alexander Carmichael's massive collection of Gaelic lore and sayings, *Carmina Gadelica,* contains invocations and phrases that can be used during your basic ritual to call on Brighid and her special power. Most of these sayings connect Brighid with the hearth and home; Brighid is always with you, especially in your home. Try to incorporate this aspect into your Practical Work. Devise a ceremony or ritual consciously acknowledging Brighid's presence in your home, and which welcomes her there. This will help to better connect your magical Work to your daily routines of cooking food, cleaning dishes, and keeping house. Brighid and the hazel will have much to tell you on these matters.

When invoking Brighid, it is helpful to keep in mind her many associations with fire and inspiration. It may be helpful to build a little fire within the confines of your Working area to give you a point of focus when you call upon Brighid to attend your Working. Many people find flames to be quite hypnotic, which can also be helpful. Most of us enjoy staring into the depths of a burning fire and letting our mind wander. It is during such spontaneous wanderings that the beings of the Otherworld find it easiest to communicate with us. If you do decide to use a living fire in your Working, be extra careful to ensure that the fire is completely out before you return home.

CHAPTER FOURTEEN

APPLE

Name: Queirt

Letter: Q

Ogham letter: ⅢⅡ

Textual reference: Queirt, Apple, shelter of a wild hind is an Apple tree.

Word Ogham of Morainn: CLITHCHAR BOSCILL, shelter of a hind, BOSCELL equals lunatic, BAS CEALL equals death sense, the time when a lunatic's senses come back to him. Therefore CLITHCHAR mBAISCAILL means shelter of lunatics.

Word Ogham of Cuchulain: DIGHU FETHAIL .i. CUMDAIGH, excellent emblem, protection.

Word Ogham of Aonghus: BRIG ANDUINE, force of a man.

Physical Level

There are many varieties of apple tree, but all of these hybrids owe their existence to the original, native, crab apple. This tree still grows in Britain, but is much neglected in favor of the larger, hybrid trees. The crab apple is a small tree, rarely more than thirty feet in height. Its bark is brown and flaky, and some wild trees still bear the thorns all crab apple trees originally had. Its leaves are oval, on alternate sides of the stalk, and have pointed tips. The flowers are large and a deeper shade of pink than on hybrid apple trees. In autumn, these flowers turn into the yellow and red apples that are smaller and more bitter than cultivated apples. Despite the fruit's bitterness, it is used to make jam, jelly, and wine.

Its wood is good for both burning and carving. A poultice made from the roasted or boiled fruit relieves pains in the side and removes burn marks from the skin. The same boiled fruit, when cooled, is good for sore or inflamed eyes. The raw fruit of the hybrid trees is good for sufferers of asthma and lung congestions. It also helps to keep the bowels regular. The leaves make a very pleasant tea, and the fruit is also used to make cider, a potent, alcoholic drink. The well-known saying, "an apple a day keeps the doctor away," shows how the apple plays an important part, even in folk memory. I have also heard the saying uttered in jest followed by the condition, "but only if you throw it very hard and very accurately!" This joke is, oddly enough, given credence by a passage in the "Cattle Raid of Cooley," which describes Cuchulain attacking a foe with an apple, which he threw so hard that it flew between the shield rim and frame and took out the back of his enemy's head.

The word apple occurs in many forms in place names throughout English-speaking countries, and in common surnames such as Appleton and Appleyard.

Mental Level

The text relating to the apple tree is very obscure, but has a great deal of symbolism and magical meaning. This is appropriate, as this is a special tree whose symbolism is hidden quite deeply. One reference states that the apple is a "shelter for a wild hind." This is repeated in a second textual reference with further comments that state it is also the "shelter of lunatics." These contain double meanings that, when understood, help to make sense of this otherwise confusing description.

The word *clithchar* means "shelter," but it also means anything that is close and warm. *Baiscaill* means "hind," but it also means a cowherd. *Boscell* means "madman" or "lunatic," but it can also be broken down into two separate words, *bas* and *ceall*, which mean "death" and "sense," respectively. From this we can see that the text can be translated in several different ways: shelter of the hind; shelter of the cowherd; shelter of a lunatic; shelter of the sense of death; close, warm place of the cowherd; close, warm place of the hind; close, warm place of the madman; close, warm place of the sense of death. None of these make immediate sense unless you understand the status of cowherds and madmen in Celtic society.

To the ancient Celts, cowherds were recognized as being very important in the structure of society. All wealth was measured in terms of cattle, and the person who looked after the clan's cattle was in a position of great trust and responsibility. Other references in the Tree Ogham emphasize the importance of cattle. Rowan is "strength of cattle," and the alder, "guarding of milk." Cattle were important because they supplied milk, meat, hide, bone, and sinew, all of which were used to the fullest by the Celts.

Cowherds were also believed to have certain magical abilities. In the Irish legends, cowherds and swineherds turn into other creatures or people who play important roles. Probably the two most famous cowherds, who were originally swineherds, are Friuch and Rucht, who feature in the epic "Cattle Raid of Cooley." These two friends eventually fell out and, through the use of their magic, spent years fighting each other in various shapes and forms—birds of prey, sea creatures, stags, warriors, phantoms, dragons, maggots, and finally the two great bulls, the Brown Bull Cuailnge and the White Bull Finnbennach. These became the center of the great cattle raid itself.

Similarly, madmen held a different place in ancient Celtic society than they do today. Their madness was believed to be a gift from the gods, and was not looked upon as a disability. The Celtic shamen, who traveled to the Otherworld on behalf of the clan, were considered to be mad in the divine sense. They often dwelled in the forest, among the trees and wild beasts, where they learned to tune into the vibrations and life forces of the Green World. They were also believed to be able to take on the shape of the animals and birds, and could become any living thing they wished.

The reference to the wild hind may actually be a reference to a shape-shifting shaman. One such wild man was Suibhne Geilt, Sweeney the Mad, who has been equated with those other great shamen from mythology, Taliesin and Merlin, as well as the lesser known Scottish wild man, Lailoken. Sweeney is a useful figure for our study and I have devoted a chapter to him later in the book. Shamen and poets carried apple branches as symbols of their office. These were known as *Craobh Ciuil*, which may mean something like "Branch of Reason." They are always identified in the legends as being apple branches.

The apple tree has very close links with the magician, or shaman, and is a tree used by him or her when undergoing magical transformations or Otherworld journeys. In legend, Otherworld visitors to this world often appear in the same guise as the shaman, carrying a branch from an apple tree with bells on it. In the "Voyage of Bran, Son of Feabhail," a woman of the Otherworld appears bearing an apple branch, speaking to Bran of the beauties and wonders of the Otherworld. So entranced is Bran that he immediately sets sail for this wondrous place and has many adventures along the way. It is this symbolic apple branch that the Word Ogham of Cuchulain refers to when he describes the apple as an "excellent emblem," a sign of "protection." The more you travel in the Otherworld, and the more you get to know its inhabitants, the more you will realize the truth of this statement.

In a description of King Conchobhar mac Neasa's palace in the "Cattle Raid of Cooley," it states that hanging over Conchobhar's head was a rod of silver with three apples of gold for keeping order over the throng. When he shook it, everyone fell into such a respectful silence you would hear a needle drop to the floor. The fact that the ancient Celts actually used symbolic trees and branches for ritualistic purposes has been authenticated by an archaeological find at Manching, in Bavaria, where a small ritual tree, seventy centimeters high, was found. It is made from wood covered in bronze and gold. On it are leaves, fruit, and berries also made entirely from bronze and gold.

The Word Ogham of Morainn, "death...when a lunatic's senses come back to him," is a reference to the magician's ability to travel to the Otherworld. By so doing, the magician dies in this world, but gains the use of his or her Otherworld senses, which are clearer and more perceptive than the senses of this world. The use of the phrase, "when a lunatic's senses come back to him," hints that these senses are already a part of you; but it is only by undergoing such an Otherworld journey that they come back to you to be put to use. Unfortunately, the converse also applies, in that these finely tuned senses close down upon returning to the denser realms of this world. The madman, lunatic, shaman, or magician is the person who is aware of both sets of senses, and who can use them as and when appropriate in both this world and the Otherworld.

The closeness, warmth, or shelter referred to by the word *clithchar* is an indication of the apple tree's receptivity to being used in such a way. It is a very powerful Otherworld symbol and, in the right hands during a ritual Working, can become a very powerful tool for use in this world as well. The sheltering aspect of the apple tree can be taken literally, in that the physical tree can be used as a shelter under which to sit when undergoing Otherworld journeys.

Spiritual Level

The apple tree is the tree you must Work with to experience the divine madness of the shaman. It is the tree to use as a calling sign to the Otherworld that you wish to enter their realm. Under the Irish system, the Otherworld has many names, and one of the more common is Avalon. This is used most frequently in the Arthurian legends, which have their basis in Celtic legend. The word itself is derived from the Old Irish word meaning "place of apple trees." The Old Irish name for the Isle of Arran in the Scottish Firth of Clyde was *Eamhain Abhlach* (evain avaloch), which means "Holy Hill of the Apple Trees." Eventually, *avaloch* became the more easily pronounced Avalon. To the Irish Celts, Eamhain Abhlach, the Isle of Arran, was believed to be the physical-level manifestation of the spiritual level, an Otherworld paradise. These associations are still given to Avalon in the surviving Arthurian legends, although its close links with the apple tree are not obvious from that body of work.

In Chapter Three, it was noted that Q was one of the three letters that were only to be used under certain circumstances. "Where C stands before U it is Queirt that is to be written there." The letter Q, however, did not and does not exist in the Irish alphabet. We know from many manuscripts that when the letters C and U occurred, they were never replaced by Q or QU, as this instruction suggests. It seems, then, that the meaning behind this pointless rule is to be found on a higher level, which is often the case when something appears confusing or meaningless on the physical or mental levels.

The two letters C and U together form the word *cu*, which means "wolf" or "hound." This was a synonym for "warrior," as in Cuchulain, Hound of Culain or Warrior of Culain. The word *cu* therefore occurs many times in the legends, as most of the legends are about warriors. When you write or read the word for warrior, *cu*, you should mentally substitute *Queirt*, and understand that the warrior's actions can be interpreted on the mental and spiritual levels as well as on the physical level. The Irish Celtic warriors were highly trained in magical and spiritual skills. Being able to read between the lines of the legends reveals practical information within what may appear to be no more than the brutal deeds of long-dead Celtic warriors.

The value of the apple tree, then, is as a spiritual warrior who is unafraid to face death or travel to the Otherworld to defend or aid his or her people. It is a tree symbolizing the hardship, sacrifice, and self-denial that the warrior/magician has to undergo to make the journey to Avalon and back. This is the "force of a man" referred to in the Word Ogham of Aonghus. The apple tree is his or her calling sign upon arrival, and is the shelter under which to rest upon return.

Practical Work

Get to know the apple on an individual basis, as you have been doing with all of the other trees. First, make your Ogham stick, then use it as a Magical Tool to help you physically, mentally, and spiritually connect with an apple tree. You can aid this process by eating apples, apple pies, and taking the occasional glass of cider. If you have the space in your garden, you could try cultivating apple trees from seed. This will give you a special link with the tree, just as eating hazelnuts did in the last chapter.

Once you have achieved some recognition from the tree, and Inner dialogue has commenced, bring in the four trees previous to the apple, just as you did in Chapter Nine with the ash. Walk again through an Otherworld forest dominated by the five trees. Note how they shift and change according to how they are placed in relation to one another. Bring in the Ogham sticks for the first five trees and mix them with your latest five. Once you feel familiar with all ten, start an Otherworld journey incorporating into the scenery all the trees examined so far.

This is the only way to really get to know the trees and how they work with one another. Take as much time as you need, for it may seem a daunting task, and more an exercise of memory than magic; but if you have been developing a personal relationship with each tree, then each will speak to you when you bring it to the fore in your visual imagination. You should not need to wrack your brains to recall symbolism and associations. Remember to record all that you do and experience in your magical diary.

The emphasis on madness associated with the apple may be uncomfortable for some people. If you have misgivings about invoking a tree spirit associated with madness, then you might benefit by reading the works of Fiona Macleod. Most of her books are out of print, having been published in the 1800s, but they are worth searching out in your local library or antiquarian book store. In many of her stories, Fiona Macleod deals with the subject of madness as understood through tree magic, and her writings provide enlightened insight into the whole question of divine spiritual madness. (It is interesting to note that Fiona, who was really a man by the name of William Sharp, did much of her writing on the Scottish Isle of Arran.) Spend some time noting your reactions to madness in your family, community, or society. We all probably know someone who is considered to be a bit odd, if not fully insane, and most city dwellers see people—often sad, homeless, and destitute people—strolling the streets in an apparent trance. Consider these people, and think about their state of mind. How did they get like that? How do you react to them? Do you cross the road, hide in a shop doorway, or do you show them the same courtesies and politeness that you (should) show everyone else? There is a lot to be learned from such casual observations and self-examinations.

Once the intricacies and complexities of the apple tree and its relationship with other trees have been studied, you must progress to the next tree. Strictly speaking, this is not a tree at all, but it still takes a good deal of understanding and unraveling, for it is the ever-entwining vine.

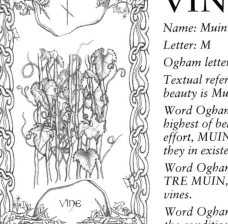

CHAPTER FIFTEEN

VINE

Name: Muin

Letter: M

Ogham letter:

Textual reference: Muin is a vine tree highest of beauty is Muin because it grows aloft.

Word Ogham of Morainn: ARDAM MAISI, highest of beauty, TRESIM FEDMA, strongest of effort, MUIN equals back of man or ox for it is they in existence that are strongest as regards effort.

Word Ogham of Cuchulain: CONAIR GOTHA .i. TRE MUIN, pack of wolves with spears, three vines.

Word Ogham of Aonghus: MARUSC N-AIRLIG, the condition of slaughter.

Physical Level

The straggling shape of the vine is familiar to people throughout the world. Despite its preference for hotter climates, it can and does grow successfully in the British Isles. It should be remembered that the origins of our Tree Ogham stretch far back in time, when the climate of the British Isles may have been much warmer than it is today. If unhindered, the vine can grow to a considerable size and develop a rough, brown bark. It has many long, meandering branches, which are incapable of supporting their own weight, and relies on long, thin, but strong tendrils, which sprout from the main stem and entwine themselves around trees and other structures. The leaves are large and round, with four or five lobes,

147

and notched at the edges. The flowers are small and greenish-white, and the roots are long and tough.

The fruit of the vine is the grape, which can be used in a variety of ways and for a variety of purposes. The dried fruit, in the form of currants or raisins, is good for coughs and chest disorders. The fermented fruit, in the form of wine or brandy, is good for calming distraught nerves, aiding digestion, inducing a sense of well-being, and is a pleasant tonic if taken in moderation. An excess of the fermented fruit is to be avoided. The boiled leaves make a good lotion for sore mouths, as well as being a soothing poultice for inflammations and wounds. A decoction of the leaves is good for helping to get rid of stones in the kidneys or bladder.

The leaves contain as many mineral salts and vitamins as do the grapes, and adding a few raw leaves to your daily diet is a habit to be encouraged. They are very good at clearing up skin conditions, calming nerves, and are a good tonic for the blood. The ash of the burned branches makes a good toothpaste, which helps to remove stains from blackened teeth. The vine's long, woody roots can be twisted and plaited into strong ropes and twines. It is a very useful plant overall, but one whose full properties and virtues are often ignored in favor of its fruit alone.

Mental Level

The Word Ogham of Morainn refers to the vine as "highest of beauty" and "strongest of effort," which means that the vine can grow higher than the host plant to which it attaches itself. It is a plant that appears to make a real effort to grow and stay aloft, meaning off the ground. The other part of this reference, "Muin equals back of man or ox for it is they in existence that are strongest as regards effort," couples the vine's great effort in growing with another meaning of *muin*, which is "back" or "top." (The word "man," in the text, means humankind, not just the male of the species.) Another meaning of the word *muin* is to "teach." This is the meaning that interests us at this level.

The vine can teach during the divine inebriation its fruit provides when used carefully. This is an extension of the properties of the apple, which is also closely connected with divine inspiration. A deeper aspect to this teaching capability is seen by studying the vine in the wild, where it uses the host tree to support its growth. This symbolizes the vine's knowledge of the properties of the host tree, and that it is in harmony and sympathy with the tree, understanding it so well that it is capable of living beside or on top of it. The vine could help us learn about the properties of other trees as well. This does not mean you have to find a vine that has twined itself around some tree before you can unravel the secrets of either; but using the vine consciously during Otherworld journeys or rituals can be an aid to new knowledge, or an alternative way to find out the properties of other trees growing in conjunction with it.

Although the fermented fruit of the vine can be a source of inspiration, this should be an act on the physical level only. It is generally inadvisable to accept offers of drink, especially intoxicating drink, when in the Otherworld. You may indeed receive divine inspiration from such Otherworld wine, but you may have to pay a high price for it. Should this situation arise during an Otherworld journey, be very careful when deciding whether to accept or to refuse. Do you know and trust the person offering the drink? Because the Otherworld part of you does not need food or drink, why is it being offered? Are you being asked to provide something in return? It is rare that such a scenario will have symbolic meaning.

The vine is a teaching tree, but it has another important function as a uniting tree. It is one of the few trees that grows in conjunction with one tree, and then spreads itself across to join another tree, and so on without limit. By doing this, it literally and symbolically unites otherwise separate trees. This is the vine's "strongest of efforts," according to the Word Ogham of Morainn. You should become like the vine by uniting the differing properties of the trees within yourself, and then turning your fruit into pleasing wine that can pass on inspiration to others. The Ogham notch for the vine is the first to straddle the central stem-line, as if the notch is meandering off in search of others upon which to rest and grow.

Spiritual Level

The vine's spiritual-level properties are very similar to its mental-level associations. It is a strong tree in that it can bind to any other tree with little resistance. You must be strong both as an individual and when living and working with others. The vine is strong in that its fruit, when fermented, can cause a person to take leave of his or her senses and, in extreme cases, die. This same fermented fruit can be the source of inspiration, and it is learning to use it properly that is the real test of this tree. Your spiritual-level Workings must achieve a balance that is neither excessive nor insufficient—the all-important state of being in-between. You should become a source of inspiration to others; for what is the point of progress and learning if you do not help others along the way?

The vine does not discriminate. In the Green World, the vine will happily attach itself to any tree that can support it. You, too, must maintain a totally unbiased attitude toward your fellow humans, and be keen to share your knowledge and experience regardless of sex, race, color, beliefs, or personality. Everyone has the right to learn, but no one has the right to withhold assistance from one who genuinely needs it.

If you have any problems with this concept, spend some time in the Otherworld Working with the vine, and study how it attaches itself and lives in harmony with other trees. The vine's Old Irish name, *Tresim Fedma*, "Strongest of Effort," is the motto you should adopt on every level.

The same points we have made about the vine can be made about most straggling or binding plants or trees, such as the bramble, another plant with fruit that can be fermented into wine. If you feel more at home Working with the bramble than with the vine, then by all means do so. During magical Workings and Otherworld journeys, it is the symbolic meaning of the tree that is important, and not how it manifests on the physical level.

We have noted the vine's connection with the apple tree, but we shall find even closer connections between the vine and the next tree.

Practical Work

It may be hard to find an appropriately shaped or sized piece of vine for your Ogham stick. You must, therefore, decide which other tree to use for this purpose. I would suggest you use wood from a tree not identified in the Tree Ogham, such as beech, chestnut, elm, or sycamore.

It may also be necessary to adapt your ritual as it is unlikely you will find a vine large enough to connect with in the same way as you have with the larger, thicker-trunked trees. Try imagining yourself to *be* the vine, the link between the trees. Go through all of the trees you have linked with so far, repeating the ritual as before, but this time as a vine slowly but steadily wrapping itself around the host tree. Place your vine Ogham stick in the ground, hold it, and simultaneously hold the host tree. Listen to the vine and to the host tree, and don't be afraid to ask your guide for help in understanding what you hear.

You may find it illuminating to consider yourself to be a vine while going about your day-to-day life—interacting with family, friends, and colleagues, walking in the park, driving the car, or sitting at work. Bring your knowledge of the trees into your daily routine, and see yourself linking and binding just like the vine as you make yourself aware of the spiritual aspect of your work.

Become aware of your multiple relationships with people, and how they weave and twist their way through your life just as the vine weaves and twists its way through the forest.

Experiment with the fruit of the vine by eating grapes and their equally nutritious leaves. Try a little wine, but be careful. A little wine can lead to divine inspiration; too much can lead to a Hellish hangover!

This is a good time to make yourself a sacred cord to wear around your waist as you carry out your ritual. This signifies to the Otherworld that you have reached an advanced stage in your tree-magic studies. It also helps to link you symbolically with the many people who have studied, who are currently studying, and who will eventually study tree magic. This cord should be long enough to wrap around your waist, tie in a knot, and still have a little left to hang loosely at your side. It can be of any material and color you choose. It is your cord, and such aesthetics are entirely up to you. Once you have found, made, or bought a suitable cord, consecrate it as you see fit. Wear your cord only during ritual or magical Workings; it is not intended to be an item of daily dress.

As the vine is the eleventh tree in the Tree Ogham, tie eleven knots along the length of your cord. From now on, as you complete each tree ritual, tie another knot in this cord, and let it serve as another mnemonic device in later Workings, where feeling its length will bring to mind the name, order, and meaning of each tree.

CHAPTER SIXTEEN

IVY

Name: Gort

Letter: G

Ogham letter:

Textual reference: Gort, that is Ivy, greener than pastures is Ivy.

Word Ogham of Morainn: GLAISEM GELTA, greenest of pastures, MILLSIU FERAIB, sweeter than grasses, due to associations with corn fields.

Word Ogham of Cuchulain: SASADH ILE .i. ARBHAR, pleasing oil, corn.

Word Ogham of Aonghus: MED NERCC, size of a warrior.

Physical Level

Ivy is another letter of the Tree Ogham that would not normally be considered a tree proper. Like the vine, it often depends upon a host tree for support, and is another binding and uniting plant. Most people are familiar with the physical appearance of the ivy, which is found in many regions growing on trees, buildings, and other structures. Its leaves are deep green and waxy, with four or five pointed lobes. The long, spindly stems are thin and slightly hairy, and grow quickly, soon covering the entire supporting tree or building. It has thin tendrils that clutch surfaces and are strong enough to force their way into plaster and brickwork, sometimes causing structural damage. When the host is a tree, it is not

153

unusual for the ivy to grow so thick that it eventually smothers and kills it. It is another evergreen, like its mate in the old Christmas carol, "The Holly and the Ivy," and is a persistent and enduring plant.

The berries of the ivy have medicinal properties, but must be taken with caution; they can be poisonous in too large a dose. Seek expert advice before attempting any self-help or healing using the ivy taken internally. The plant has several safe uses if applied externally. A brew of fresh leaves boiled in vinegar and pressed against the aching area is a good source of relief for pains such as a stitch or a headache. A similar potion of fresh leaves is good for cleaning wounds or sores on any part of the body. A powder made from the dried leaves and berries can be used sparingly as snuff to clear blocked noses and stuffy heads. It is also believed to be a good cure for a hangover, which links it magically to the vine and its intoxicating properties. Remember, just as with the vine, moderation must be applied. Ivy is a common personal name among English-speaking peoples.

Mental Level

The Word Ogham of Morainn refers to ivy as "greenest of pastures" and "sweeter than grasses." This is yet again a play on words, this time on the word *gort*, which means "green field" or "garden." It also means "standing corn," and hence, the reference to corn fields in the Word Ogham. The ivy plant and the honeysuckle, or woodbine, are interchangeable in legends and poetry. The word honeysuckle would seem to be implied in the description "sweeter than grasses." The importance of the ivy or honeysuckle from a magical point of view is that, although it seems to be very similar to the vine, it is actually stronger; the vine rarely kills its host, but the ivy, more often than not, does.

Because of this ability to kill even the mighty oak, the ivy is regarded as a very powerful tree indeed. Its ability to bind together the trees of the forest and create dense, impenetrable thickets give it an air of malice. The Ogham notch used to represent the ivy is two lines crossing the central stem, twice the number used to represent the vine. This shows that the ivy is even more capable than the vine of spreading itself to bind its host tree or trees.

Just as you should be cautious with the ivy on the physical level, so should you exercise care when on the magical level. There may be a hint of this in a description of the boyhood deeds of Fionn mac Cumhaill from the *Lays of Fionn:*

> In a hollow of a tall ivy-clad tree is nursed that noble Fiann leader. One day he is left alone and a polecat passes near the hollow. It comes for the infant with no terror. He closes his grasp round the polecat and he keeps choking it from early morn until eve.[1]

It is not a tree you would consciously use during Otherworld journeys; you would not wish to get yourself into a thicket, or find yourself bound and restricted to the point of suffocation. It is a useful tree, however, for those in the Otherworld who have your interests at heart, and who may wish to point out that you are going in the wrong direction. They do this by placing a dense thicket of ivy or honeysuckle in your way during an Otherworld journey. Should this occur, you would be advised to stop and think seriously about what you are trying to achieve. This sudden appearance may indicate that your whole intention is wrong, and needs to change or to be abandoned altogether.

The ivy is a tree you should hope not to encounter often in your magical studies. If you find it cropping up with frequency, I would suggest that you cease all Otherworld and magical Work until you have had the chance to review your reasons for taking up this

---

[1] Gerard Murphy, trans., *Duanaire Finn* (Dublin: Irish Texts Society, 1933).

course of study and development. You should also take a good look at your physical-level life. Once you have identified the cause of the problem and taken the necessary remedial steps, you can safely resume your journey through the forest of the Tree Ogham. The positive aspects of the ivy—pleasing oil and being sweeter than grasses—become more meaningful to you once you realize you have narrowly averted danger thanks to the warning of the ivy tree.

Spiritual Level

The spiritual lesson to be learned from the ivy is that you are not always as in control as you may think. At times it will take others, whether of this world or the Otherworld, to point out the dangers you are about to encounter or the mistakes you are about to make. At this advanced stage in your progress, you may feel that you are beyond such dangers and no longer likely to make mistakes. The truth is that you are in more danger than you were during your early sojourns into these new and fascinating realms. When you first attempt magical Work, you are incapable of anything that could cause harm. Even then, there were always watchful eyes keeping your interests at heart. Once you learn, progress, and develop your abilities, you gain powers and skills that could be used incorrectly or indiscreetly. With this comes the responsibility and accountability for their use. Even though your unseen Otherworld friends, guides, and guardians are there, they become less and less inclined to step in and steer you away from harm. The onus lies with you to explain your actions and intentions. Not having made too many mistakes of a serious nature by this point, you may tend to become too self-assured and exhilarated by your new powers and abilities. This is when you can unwittingly become a danger to yourself and to others.

No matter how big and strong you think you are, the puny little ivy that, as the Word Ogham of Aonghus says, is the "size of a warrior," can still take hold of you, gently at first, and slowly bind and restrict you. The ivy will make you stop to examine what you are doing and your motives for doing it. Should you be unable or refuse to see the error of your ways, it will squeeze you until you are no longer capable of doing anything.

Meditation on what you have achieved, how you have behaved, how you see yourself, and whether you still realize the need for discretion is the subject for the spiritual level of the ivy.

Practical Work

As with the vine, I would suggest you try experiencing what it is like to actually be the ivy. See how it feels to bind tightly around the other trees, and learn what this means on the physical level in your daily life. The ivy is a warning tree. Where and when do you give warnings during your normal day-to-day business? Are you conscious of doing this at all? Are your warnings heeded? Are they always right and necessary? Do you heed warnings that are given to you by other people?

At this point in your progress and magical Workings, it may be a good idea to take a break. Carry on studying this book, but take some time out from the Practical Work. Magical exercises require rest periods, just as physical exercises do. During this rest period, reflect on how things have gone so far. Read your magical diary to see patterns forming and progress you have made. Look at the Green World around you with new eyes, and see yourself as intimately connected with all the myriad of life forms, not just with the trees. Feel at one with it and rejoice in the realization.

Spend some time playing with your Ogham sticks. Hold them. Study them. See how easily the names of the trees come to you just by looking at the notches on your sticks. How much symbolism leaps to mind as you do this? Are there some concepts that come more easily than others? See this as a form of relaxation, like playing cards. When you feel sufficiently refreshed and ready to press on, then reread the next chapter (assuming you have already read to the end of the book), and study carefully what is said there.

CHAPTER SEVENTEEN

BROOM

Name: nGetal

Letter: nG

Ogham letter:

Textual reference: nGetal, broom or fern, a physician's strength is broom.

Word Ogham of Morainn: LUTH LEIGHE, a physician's strength, CATH equals panacea. GETAL equals broom.

Word Ogham of Cuchulain: TOSACH N-ECHTO .i. ICCE, beginning of heroic deeds, healing.

Word Ogham of Aonghus: EITIUD MIDACH, robe of physicians.

Physical Level

The yellow-flowered broom grows in all parts of the British Isles and is a familiar sight along the heaths, moors, and open spaces. It rarely grows higher than about seven feet, but what it lacks in height it makes up for in width, being an exceptionally bushy shrub. It has long, thin, green stalks, which host a profusion of golden, pod-shaped flowers in the summer months. Its main stem can grow quite thick, and is green but more scaly than the many stalks. It is related to the gorse bush, which is similar in appearance, although the gorse is armed with long, sharp spines, and flowers more times per year than the broom.

The broom has many uses and, as the name suggests, its long, flexible stems were often tied into a besom and used as a broom about the house. A decoction of the young branches or seeds will cause violent vomiting if taken in too strong a dose or too large a measure, but a controlled intake is good at relieving conditions such as gout, sciatica, and painful joints. It affords relief to those who suffer from recurring bouts of malaria or fever. It is also a diuretic, and helps to break down stones in the kidneys and bladder. Oil can be drawn from the stems by heating them over an open fire, and this tincture is good for relieving toothaches. The same oil, if boiled and allowed to cool, is good at cleansing the head and skin of parasites such as lice.

The wood of its close cousin, the gorse, burns very well, as do the stalks and spines themselves, but it is not a plant that you would think of cultivating just for its timber. Gorse is a very hardy plant and a great colonizer, and is exceedingly difficult to get rid of once it takes root. In the past, it was planted and shaped into hedgerows, and most old houses had at least one large gorse bush in the garden that was used to dry laundry, its spines stopping the drying clothes from blowing away.

By tradition, the Traveling People of Scotland and Ireland camp in one location throughout the cold winter. Come summer, they break camp and spend the warmer months traveling from village to village and from island to island. The time to break winter camp is not determined by the calendar, but by the first yellow flowers of the broom. In other words, it is the Green World that notifies the impending change in the weather and the time to start traveling again. This heralding of new beginnings also applies to the non-physical levels.

The word broom still appears in several surnames, as well as in common place names such as Broomhill and Broomfield.

Mental Level

nGetal is similar to the letter *Queirt* in that it is one of the three composite letters to be used only in certain circumstances. *Queirt*, according to the text, is to be used when U follows C, and *nGetal* is to be used only when N stands before G. It was noted earlier that, despite this grammatical rule, the letter *Queirt* is never found in the written manuscripts. Its real use is, instead, on a higher level. So, too, with *nGetal*.

To gain an understanding of the higher aspects of this composite letter, first remind yourself of the properties of the individual letters N and G. You will remember that the ash symbolizes breaking free from a period of lethargy or inertia. When this is achieved, there will be a backlash. We also know that the letter *Gort*, the ivy, is a cautionary tree whose presence should be carefully noted during Workings. *nGetal* then, being a combination of the letters N and G, the ash and ivy, is a letter and tree symbolizing the combined effects of these two trees.

What this means in practical terms is that, if you have started some new Work or broken a period of inactivity, and if the backlash is potentially dangerous or destructive, then the ivy will be invoked by the Otherworld to warn you. You must take note of this and abandon the new Work. It would be dangerous, however, to simply stop the Work without checking to see if there is repair or healing needed due to damage already caused. The broom is the tree that should be used in such circumstances to "clean up" the damage done. This is exactly the way you use a broom on the physical level, and for exactly the same reasons. The broom is correcting, or healing, any damage or injury inadvertently caused. Its title in the Word Ogham of Morainn, "physician's strength, panacea," reflects this, as does its title in the Word Ogham of Cuchulain, "beginning of heroic deeds, healing," and again in the Word Ogham of Aonghus, "robe of physicians." Magical hygiene is as important as physical hygiene. To leave things lying around half done on a magical level can cause infection and disease. Independent life forms can attach themselves to things left by careless Otherworld travelers. These Otherworld "viruses" can take on a life of their own, and do considerable damage.

In the higher realms, these unwanted items, dirt if you will, may not be obvious. They can consist of abstract things such as incorrect or malicious thoughts, feelings, emotions, and mental actions. You must learn to recognize them, and this is what the ivy will help you do. Then you must learn to use the broom as your inner sight and smell to pick up these things and get rid of them.

The simple broom is an important tree, but one you should not need too often. If you are ever not sure whether you need it, always play it safe and use it anyway. It is a panacea, as the Word Ogham of Morainn says.

Spiritual Level

What has been said about the properties and symbolism of the broom on the physical and mental levels applies equally to the spiritual level. You must be as cautious about hygiene on this level as you are on the others. It could be argued that the need for the cleansing and healing of the broom is even more important on this level, as anything occurring here—positive or negative—will inevitably have a physical and mental-level effect as well. The spiritual message of the broom is that, if you have had to use it on any level, spend some time checking your spiritual level for damage that must be cleansed or healed. Reflect on what went wrong, and why the ivy and the broom had to be invoked in the first place. Take the opportunity to learn from your mistakes in your magical and spiritual Workings.

This is what the Word Ogham of Cuchulain means when it refers to using the broom as "beginning of heroic deeds." True heroes were skilled in not only the physical arts of war and combat, but also in the higher, magical arts. This sometimes means recognizing things about yourself—your feelings, thoughts, and emotions—which might actually be dangerous or damaging, and which must be dealt with. This can be an unpleasant experience, and to do this is indeed the beginning of heroic deeds.

Practical Work

If you can find a long, straight, and thick enough piece of broom from which to make your Ogham stick, that is ideal; but it is rare for broom to grow to such a thickness, so look for a substitute if need be.

It should be possible for you to find a suitable broom for your tree ritual, but should this become a problem, it may be helpful to perform the adaptation mentioned in the previous two chapters. Spend some time alternating between these two approaches. First, make an effort to connect with the broom by carrying out the basic ritual, and invoking the Daghdha and your guide. Next, carry out the ritual by imagining yourself as the broom, and seeing how you react when linking with the other trees. Examining these two different aspects of the broom and how they manifest within you will help you appreciate exactly what the broom will mean to you when it appears during Otherworld journeys.

Try linking the broom with the ash and the ivy. These are the two trees for the letters N and G that, according to the textual references, are the trees (letters) to be used when *nGetal* appears. By linking these trees during your basic ritual, you will feel how they shift and change when placed next to each other. Do this by placing your Ogham stick in the ground and then linking with your broom tree. Once you have established the link, place your broom Ogham stick in the ground while linking with your ash tree. Once you have a reaction, change from your ash to your ivy.

The next stage is to take your ash Ogham stick, place it in the ground and link with broom and ivy, and finally, place your ivy stick in the ground and link with broom and ash. This is going to take you some time, but if you wish to learn the language of the trees fully and completely, the rewards of these actions will be well worth it.

Now would be a good time to embark on a physical cleaning of your living area. This chore can be made magical simply by regarding it as such. It is a conscious and physical act designed to cleanse not only your home, but your Higher Self. By using a physical broom on the physical level, with this magical intention, you will be linking the spiritual and physical levels together, with results on both. You could also perform an Otherworld journey at this stage, specifically designed to help you recognize and deal with subtle aspects of your Self that may need "sweeping up" spiritually. Your guide should prove valuable in noticing aspects of your personality that need some attention.

CHAPTER EIGHTEEN

BLACKTHORN

Name: Straiph

Letter: St

Ogham letter:

Textual reference: Straiph, that is Blackthorn, the hedge of a stream is Sraiph.

Word Ogham of Morainn: AIRE SRABHA, careful effort, TRESIM RUAMNA, strongest of red. STRAIPH equals sloe which gives strong red dye on metal.

Word Ogham of Cuchulain: SAIGID NEL .I. A DDE SUAS, an arrow's mist, smoke drifting up from the fire.

Word Ogham of Aonghus: MORAD RUN, increasing of secrets.

Physical Level

The blackthorn is more a large shrub than a tree, and rarely reaches its full height of thirteen feet. It is found throughout the British Isles, usually on the edge of woodlands or in old hedgerows. It is covered with strong, sharp thorns, and grows into a dense, knotted, impenetrable thicket, which is a favorite nesting place for birds. Its leaves are small, oval-shaped, dull on top and hairy underneath, and on alternate sides of the stalk. It has white flowers with five petals with little red tips. Its bark is rough and scaly, and is bright orange just under the gray surface. The light-yellow sapwood and brown heartwood are not used a great deal, as the tree never grows big enough to

165

be of any commercial value. Its main uses are in marquetry and the manufacture of walking sticks. It is the traditional wood for making the Irish shillelagh.

Its fruit is the round, shiny, deep-purple berries known as sloes. The fruit is used in jam and in flavoring gin to produce the famous sloe-gin. It is very bitter, but is a good astringent and can stop both internal and external hemorrhages. The leaves can be boiled into a decoction that, once cooled, is an excellent mouthwash and gargle for those suffering from tonsillitis or laryngitis. It can also be used as a soothing eye bath. A tea made from the powdered bark has a calming effect on the nerves. The dark juice of the sloe can be used as an ink that is difficult to erase or remove, especially from cloth.

Mental Level

This letter is the last of the letters used in letter combinations. In this case, the text tells us that "where S stands before D it is *Straiph* that is to be written," but, as with the other double letters, this is never found in the manuscripts themselves. The correctness of this use is further called into question by the variety of spellings for the letter in the written sources. It does help, however, to remember what we know about the interchangeability of the letters D and T. The text tells us that *Straiph* is to be used when S precedes D, but it is the letter T which is combined with S to make up the name of the letter.

In *Straiph,* we have S, the willow, combining with D, the oak, or perhaps T, the holly, which together are represented by the blackthorn. The titles given in the Word Ogham of Morainn for the blackthorn, "careful effort, strongest of red," "strong red dye on metal," and in the textual reference, "the hedge of a stream," are all to do with death and warriors. The color red is always synonymous with death in the Irish legends; in fact, the two words are interchangeable. The strong red dye on metal is blood on the warrior's sword. The hedge of a stream is a description of tightly bunched warriors' spears (the hedge) as they advanced (the stream). These associations appear in a passage from one version of the "Cattle Raid of Cooley," which contains a warning to Cuchulain not to advance:

> Your red-plagued blood will drip
>
> from numerous splintered shields.
>
> The army which will swarm with fires
>
> is a legion which they lead in many companies.
>
> A torrent of blood will be showered
>
> over Cuchulain as well as flesh.
>
> You will suffer from a wound of vengeance,
>
> afflicted from encounters with a hedge of spears.
>
> By an iron point will the red shield be splintered,
>
> blazing against pierced skin.[1]

The two letters and trees that make up *Straiph* are also enlightening. The willow was described as the color of a lifeless one and hue of the lifeless, owing to the resemblance of its color to a dead person. These descriptions seem to correspond to the ideas being portrayed above. The oak was described as being a shelter or protection for warriors, and the holly was the substitute for the real king, who was expected to lay down his life on behalf of his people. From this combination of images and ideas, you can see that the significance of the blackthorn at this level is really quite deep, and must be fully understood before you will be able to make any use of it.

If you turn to the legends for guidance, which is always a wise move, you will find in the "Pursuit of Diarmaid and Grainne" a passage describing the woman, Sadhbh, eating the fruit from a

---

[1] Cecile O'Rahilly, *Tain Bo Cuailgne* (Dublin: Irish Texts Society, 1962).

blackthorn tree, becoming pregnant, and giving birth to a son with a curious lump across his head. It turns out that this lump was a worm, or snake, which is eventually killed in compensation for another man's life. In the *Lays of Fionn,* there is a strange poem called "The Sword of Oscar" that mingles classical mythology with Irish mythology. Sloe berries are introduced again, as are the themes of one person dying on behalf of another.

What this tree represents is the warrior's death in the service of his or her High King, and on behalf of his or her people. The references in the Word Ogham of Cuchulain, "an arrow's mist," and "smoke drifting up from the fire," are kennings for death. If you substitute the word magician for warrior in the above comments, you will have a description of the blackthorn's meaning for you. It is facing up to your own death, whether it be soon or a long way away, violent or peaceful. Sooner or later you are going to face the transition from this world to the Otherworld; it is best to be prepared, rather than go kicking and screaming, just as you arrived. Contemplating and meditating on your own death is not as morbid as it may first appear. It is a practice used by many magical and spiritual disciplines, only neglected by the Christian Church in the West, contributing to the fear of death and dying.

It is inadvisable to visualize your own death during an Otherworld journey. The effects of this action could be traumatic. This is what the Word Ogham of Morainn means by "careful effort." You must always remember that these journeys are real; they are actually happening in the Otherworld. Visualizing yourself dying, no matter how calmly or peacefully, is clearly not a good idea. It is acceptable, however, to consider the effects of your death, not the death itself, on you and those you leave behind. If you find it difficult to do this, use the fruit of the blackthorn, or hold a branch or spray of its flowers, to help. As the Word Ogham of Aonghus tells us, the blackthorn is also the "increasing of secrets." This mental exercise, involving the powers of the blackthorn, can be quite illuminating. Most people have never fully considered the ongoing effects of their own death. A lot of people have probably given it no more than a cursory thought, and have taken out life insurance for the financial well-being of any surviving family. This is not the same thing. Most people confess to a belief in some sort of life after death, but very few have considered in-depth what this actually means for them, shifting their sphere of existence from this world to the Otherworld. Death is the only future event we can say with certainty will happen to us all. It makes sense to come to a personal understanding of what it is going to mean to you as an individual, and to prepare for it.

Spiritual Level

The spiritual lesson of the blackthorn is to accept the inevitability of your own death, and to prepare for it. This means having a good grasp of what the Otherworld is and what it means to you. It also means more mundane things like making sure all of your debts, on all levels, are paid; that there is nothing left unsaid or undone in this world; that provision has been made for those you leave behind; and that you are ready and able to face those who have gone before you. These will include friends and family whom you will be pleased to rejoin; but there will also be those whom you tried to avoid in this world. You must be in a constant state of readiness for death, doing things as soon as they need to be done, saying things when they need to be said, and repaying debts and favors as soon as practical. Tomorrow may be too late.

You can try to examine your death objectively by seeing yourself as a sort of Otherworld judge, who is now reviewing your physical life and deciding just how you coped with it.[2] Use your

---

[2] This is not to imply that there are such things as Otherworld judges; under the Irish system there is no concept of reward or punishment for deeds done in this world. There is no concept such as the Christian doctrine of Sin or the Hindu belief in Karma.

imagination at a spiritual level to scrutinize how you have fared in this world so far. Act upon any faults or omissions you identify during such spiritual exercises. Use the spirit of the blackthorn to help you through these difficult exercises. They will leave an indelible mark in your aura, just as the juice of the sloe will upon your clothes. This mark will point out, to those who can see such things, that you are a person who understands the nature of this world and the Otherworld, and who is not afraid to move from one to the other as the need demands.

Practical Work

Working through the tree ritual, and creating your own blackthorn Ogham stick, will give you a clearer view of your place in the scheme of things, and a clearer understanding of what your own death will mean to you, your family, and friends. During your Practical Work, you may find it helpful to call upon the Irish Celtic god Donn. Donn is very closely associated with death, and he will explain things and remove much of the mystery associated with death and dying. He is also a father figure, a helping, guiding, and protecting deity. To the ancient Celts, Donn was the collective father, the death from which we were born and to which we shall return. Seeing death in this parental role helps to defuse any sense of terror and fright.

You may experience some odd and upsetting reactions as a result of the Practical Work connected to this tree. Do not worry. You are dealing with something most people spend their lives repressing until literally the last minute. Once you have faced this, it will become merely another facet of life and living.

Once again, try performing the basic ritual with the other two Ogham sticks relevant to the blackthorn—the willow and the oak/holly. By linking through the different sticks to the different trees, you will be building up some practical experience and knowledge of how the trees relate and interact or react with one another. This extra facet to your basic ritual will take time, but these things cannot be rushed. By their very nature they take a long time to become a conscious and working part of your Otherworld Self.

Remember, as always, after completing the basic ritual, to record ideas, thoughts, and realizations in your magical diary. You will find that, as you progress, these ideas will start to change with your understanding of the nature of the trees and their links with the Otherworld. The blackthorn is a good tree to return to now and again to see how you are progressing, and how your understanding is changing.

CHAPTER NINETEEN

ELDER

Name: Ruis
Letter: R
Ogham letter: ⪫⪫⪫⪫
Textual reference: Ruis is Elder, the redness of shame.
Word Ogham of Morainn: TINNEM RUICE, intensest of blushes, it is reddening of a man's face through the juice of the herb being rubbed on it.
Word Ogham of Cuchulain: BRUTH FERGGA .i. IMDERGADH, arduous anger, punishment.
Word Ogham of Aonghus: ROMNAD DRECH, redness of faces.

Physical Level

Given room and light, the elder tree can grow to thirty feet in height. Its bark is light brown, thick, and covered in deep ridges and grooves. Its leaves are broadly oval shaped, on alternate sides of the knobby stalk, and usually in groups of five to seven. The flowers are very small, creamy white, with five petals and a strong sweet scent.

In autumn, the elder is covered in bunches of black berries, which have a variety of uses. The berries and the leaves are used in wine and jam. Both are rich in vitamin C. A tea made from the flowers is good for the treatment of coughs and irritating throat conditions. A shampoo made from the boiled berries has the effect of darkening the hair, as well as cleaning it. The boiled leaves, if mixed with olive oil and allowed to cool, are an excellent drop for inflammation or pain in the ears. A distillation made from the flowers is a good skin cleanser, a cure for headaches and the common cold, and an excellent tonic for the blood. The bark of the smaller and newer twigs can be dried and administered as a laxative. Various parts of the tree can be used to obtain different colored dyes. The bark provides a deep, black dye, the leaves a rich green, and the flowers, blue or lilac dyes. The stems have a soft center that can be hollowed out to make whistles, pea-shooters, and pop-guns for the amusement of children and adults alike.

Elder is a common English-language surname, but this may derive not from the tree, but rather from the position within the church hierarchy or some other ancient social structure. It is quite fitting that the elder tree should be the last in our list of consonants.

Mental Level

It may seem from the chapter on the blackthorn that, once you have faced up to your own death, there is nothing left to do. Acknowledging your own physical death is an important part of your whole experience, but death is not the end, it is merely a transformation from one type of existence to another. It is necessary to consider other aspects of physical death for you and for those who survive you in this world. To the ancient Celts, and to many other races today, it is considered vital to have a good reputation for being brave, honorable, and, above all, truthful. The image others have of you is not only necessary during your lifetime in this world, but has to remain so after your physical death. It is of the utmost importance that you are seen to die honorably and bravely. To live a life of honor, bravery, and truth, but to blow the whole thing at the last minute by dying a coward, was considered to be a dreadful thing by the Celts of old.

Some of the world's ancient civilizations believed that, to continue to exist in the Otherworld, it was necessary for your physical remains to be kept intact in this world, as in the case of the ancient Egyptians; or for your memory to be kept alive to give you vitality in the realms of the dead, as in the case of some Native American tribes. The ancient Celts did not see things quite this way, although their beliefs were similar. They did not feel it was necessary to preserve the body to sustain life in the Otherworld. This is evidenced by their practice of cremation. Similarly, they did not believe it was only by staying alive in the memories of the people of this world that you remained alive in the Otherworld. They did believe that, because of the strong contact between this world and the Otherworld, peoples' perceptions or memories of you in this world would affect the way you were viewed in the Otherworld. This made it vital that you be remembered as a strong, brave, and truthful person. This is still a common belief today, although in greatly simplified form. People have a desire to be remembered for the good they achieved during their lifetime, or for simply being a good person. This may also explain the very deep belief many westerners have that it is wrong to speak ill of the dead, even though most are quite happy to speak ill of the living, and often behind the subject's back.

The mental level of the elder is a meditation or contemplation on this point, which is a natural progression from the exercises of the blackthorn. The textual description of the elder, "the redness of shame," gives an indication as to the probable outcome of these thoughts and ideas. Similarly, the Word Ogham of Morainn, "intensest of blushes," and the Word Ogham of Aonghus, "redness of faces," touch on this point. More often than not, when you try to review the good and bad points of your life, it is the bad ones that seem most prominent. To overcome this, it is important to accept that you cannot change what you have already done, but you can learn from it and make sure you do not repeat these errors in the future. You can also use your mistakes in a positive way by admitting them to yourself and to others and, if appropriate, by making any necessary compensation for damage done. This is the "arduous anger, punishment" to which the Word Ogham of Cuchulain refers. There is a poem from the *Lays of Fionn* called "The Headless Phantoms" in which Fionn finds himself spending the night in a strange house, where the owner is burning elder logs. Throughout the long night, Fionn is forced to face all sorts of horrible, taunting creatures. He eventually falls into a swoon and, when he awakens in the morning, the house, the owner, and the phantoms have all disappeared. This is an allegory for facing up to those aspects of yourself that you have previously tried to repress, but that, if you are to progress at all, you must challenge and deal with as necessary.

There are other things that will come to mind during the mental exercises of the elder that do not fit neatly into the above category of identifiable mistakes. These are tricky to recognize and deal with, and include such things as bias, bigotry, unfairness, selfishness, and a desire to acquire things just to have them. These must be reconciled before the blushings of the elder will go away, and you can hold your head high with confidence.

Recognizing the good things you have done, the achievements you have made, the help you have given, and so forth, is as important as acknowledging the wrong things you have done. For some curious reason, those of us who live in the western world today are discouraged from singing our own praises, as if to do so is somehow morally wrong. If praises are really due, it is a good thing to be able to admit this, at least to yourself, along with admitting the not-so-good things. There must always be balance. Having your good points recognized and praised by others can also bring on the effect of the elder, blushing and reddening of face.

Spiritual Level

The spiritual lesson of this final consonant in the Tree Ogham is the cleansing and purging needed to complete the mental exercises given above. This means that you will have to consider yourself as an individual, and also as a member of the larger groups to which you belong. These include family and social groups, as well as the racial links we all have. It is on the spiritual level that our sense of personal identity, of being one, becomes overshadowed by these greater links. You must realize that, just as these unseen historical influences determine how you develop as an individual, so, too, do you affect them and all who are members of your family, social group, or race, now and in the future. The way you are remembered will inevitably affect someone, somewhere, at some time. This is most obvious in the extreme cases of religious leaders, great philosophers, thinkers, or saints, whose lives are used as models. By the way they lived just one incarnation, they have affected people for generations to come. Not everyone will have such an affect on the future, but you will leave some mark that will be bigger than you were as an individual. Contemplating this may well lead to further reddening of the face, for it makes you very aware of how closely linked we all are. You have a responsibility for yourself and for others, and this responsibility can manifest in very subtle ways. The elder tree will help you sort this out into an understandable, acceptable, and workable scheme, which can be used to advance yourself and everyone else. The English-language name for this tree, elder, is very appropriate, for it is our elders who show us the way. One day you will be an elder for a generation yet to come. Spend some time with this tree and its lessons, for it is an important one.

Practical Work

Once you have achieved sufficient familiarity with this tree through the basic ritual, repeat the exercise involving the previous five trees as you have done before. When you have experienced the relationships between these trees, expand the exercise to incorporate all of the consonant trees. Build a forest scene where all of the species are present and interacting. Walk through this landscape and open yourself to all of the influences around you.

This completes your look at the consonants of the Tree Ogham; all that remains are the five vowels. You will note slight differences between the method of description for the consonant trees and the vowel trees as you read the following chapters. The Word Ogham descriptions of the vowel trees tend to be short statements of fact, with few of the kennings that are so numerous in the descriptions of the consonant trees. You will also notice that, on a physical level, the practical uses of each tree become fewer as you make your way to the top of the Tree Ogham. This is to be expected. You are moving farther away from the mundane level, and reaching to the highest branches of the highest trees. This also reflects the similarities between an examination of a written alphabet with its rules of spelling and grammar and an examination of our Tree Ogham, with its own peculiar rules. In most alphabets, vowels tend to be used in very different ways from consonants in the construction of words and sentences. So it is with the vowel trees and their unique instruction and guidance.

Carry out your basic ritual, and watch as you form quite an elaborate forest of trees, ideas, emotions, realizations, and symbolism, incorporating all that you have come to know so far. A firm understanding of the consonant trees is vital to appreciating the subtle aspects of the vowel trees. Put down roots, reach your branches to the sky, and let the life-force of the trees build within you at its own steady pace. You will have a lot to record in your magical diary following this exercise. Be consistent and thorough and remember to note any ideas that occur outside of your formal Practical Work sessions as well.

CHAPTER TWENTY

FIR

Name: Ailm
Letter: A
Ogham letter: ┼
Textual reference: Ailm, a Fir tree, a Pine tree.
Word Ogham of Morainn: ARDAM IACH-
TADHA, loudest of groanings, that is, wondering.
AILM or A for that is what a man says while
groaning in disease or wonder.
Word Ogham of Cuchulain: TOSACH GARMA .i.
A, beginning of the weavers' beams, ahh.
Word Ogham of Aonghus: TOSACH FREGRA,
beginning of answers.

Physical Level

The word fir means little in itself, being no more than a collective noun for various types of pine trees. Today in the British Isles, there are many different species of pine, but the only one native to these isles which would have been known to the Irish Celts is the Scots Pine. This magnificent tree can grow to one-hundred-twenty feet, and is a very impressive sight, especially if there are several trees growing together. Its bark is divided into distinct halves, with the lower trunk being covered in a reddish-brown, deeply fissured bark, while the upper trunk is brighter red with a much smoother surface. Being a pine tree, it is an evergreen, and does not have leaves as much as thin needles that

181

grow in twisted pairs. The fruit of the tree is the pine cone, which eventually opens and releases the winged seeds. Scots Pines can have cones on each branch, covering a three-year period, with new buds forming on the branch tips, and the previous years' cones slightly farther down the branch.

The wood of the fir is strong but manageable, and is used for a variety of purposes including furniture manufacture. Because of its height and straight trunk, it is popular in the construction of telephone poles and ships' masts. It is a source of turpentine, resin, and tar, as well as good quality charcoal. A tea made from the fresh shoots, if boiled gently and allowed to cool, is a good protection against urinary, kidney, and bladder infections. It is also a cure for scurvy, an illness rarely found these days. The tea also makes a soothing and refreshing bath, and can ease aching joints and limbs if gently massaged into them. An inhalation of the hot vapors is good for clearing blocked noses and sinuses.

At one time, much of Scotland was covered in these great trees, but now only a tiny fraction of the original forests remains, and only in small patches. Much of the artificially planted forests, which march across the hills and glens in great, regimented rows, consist of imported fir trees planted as cash crops. Many of these have become well-established in the British Isles, so it may be reasonable to acknowledge that, from a symbolic point of view, they could be acceptable images for use when Working with the letter *Ailm*. It is unnecessary to be concerned with the many varieties of fir in order to proceed with your Work. Go into the woods, find whatever species of fir you can, and get to know it on all three levels. If your intuition tells you that this is an acceptable tree, then that is good enough.

Mental Level

The description in the Word Ogham of Morainn, "loudest of groanings...what a man says while groaning in disease or wonder," and the reference in the Word Ogham of Aonghus to "beginning of answers," are all based on a principle that still applies today. The sound of the letter A, "aah," can express both amazement and wonder, as well as the experience of reaching the solution to a problem. At the other end of the scale, it can be a cry or groan indicating physical or mental pain. It is, in a sense, the opposite ends of the range of human endurance or experience. You can be in the highest ecstasies of spiritual revelation and realization, crying "aah" in divine wonder, or you can be in the depths of illness and injury, crying "aah" in agony or discomfort. The sound itself changes little, but the way in which it is uttered changes markedly, and leaves no doubt in the listener's mind as to which state the crier is in.

Just as the expression "aah" must be spoken in the correct tones to indicate in what sense it is to be understood, or must be written in a context, we must see what other tree or trees the pine is connected with in various circumstances to recognize the sense in which it means to be understood—spiritual ecstasy or physical and mental agony.

A vowel on its own means little. Its sense and pronunciation change, depending upon the other letters beside which it is placed. It is entirely dependent upon other letters for its existence and meaning. The tree letter, likewise, can only be understood in conjunction with other trees; and, of course, the other trees can be slightly changed in meaning by joining them to a vowel tree. You have to learn what each tree means on its own, and also how these meanings shift and change as they are linked to other trees. This is the same process we go through when learning to read and write. We begin with the alphabet, and then go on to learn how to put together the letters to produce words that are more meaningful than the sum total of their individual parts. We soon realize that, although there are rules as to which letter can or cannot go with that other letter, the possible combinations are endless. So it is with learning and understanding the Tree Ogham. Once you have learned the full meaning of the Tree Ogham, you must carry on with your studies and Otherworld Workings to make up your own tree words and sentences, and to be able to read the tree words of others.

Serious consideration of the way the same sound means different things when differently inflected is one way to understand the deeper aspects of the fir. This multiple aspect is reflected in the Green World in the more than two hundred different varieties of pine tree, all of which are basically the same thing, but all of which manifest physically in recognizably different forms.

Otherworld journeys are another means to experiment, visualizing different trees at different times of the year. Stand close to a pine or fir and contemplate how the various connections feel to you and what, if anything, happens during the Working as a result of this. Some of these results will be ecstatic, some will be painful; but you must know them to be able to Work with them at a later date.

Spiritual Level

The Old Irish name for the fir, *Ailm*, comes from a root that can mean "that which goes forward" and also "will or desire." This sums up the purpose of the mental-level exercise for this letter. It is making you break new ground, to go forth and, using your will, to experiment in new areas and see your results. This is the "beginning of the weaver's beam" referred to in the Word Ogham of Cuchulain. The weaver's beam, you will remember, is a kenning for a spear, which symbolizes the will of the magician. On a spiritual level, you can take this a step further and contemplate the broader issues involved in what happens when you place one thing next to another thing.

Consider this idea with people, including yourself. Try to see how you relate to being placed next to someone you particularly dislike, someone you love, someone you do not know very well, someone you like but who does not like you, and so on. Build a picture of just how interrelated and interdependent we are. The same thing occurs in the Green World forest. All the trees in the forest are interdependent. Whether or not they are of the same species, or are compatible with each other, they comprise a separate entity with a life and vitality of its own, that is the forest.

The pine, or fir, is the first tree encountered that, on the surface, seems vague and hard to define on the mental and spiritual levels. This does not mean it is unknowable; it will just take time. Steady work on this tree, especially at the spiritual level, will bear fruit, and will help broaden your understanding of the Tree Ogham as a whole. One day you will find yourself saying, "aah!" in sudden comprehension.

At these lofty levels in our progression through the Tree Ogham, you are beginning to be presented with abstract concepts. You will find that your ordinary mental-level logic, the part of you that controls most of your ideas and decisions, becomes useless. If you try to approach these vowel trees from a purely logical point of view, you will only baffle yourself further. What you must learn to do is listen to your intuition, the deeper, inner, more spiritual part of yourself, which you, more often than not, completely ignore. Intuition only takes over your consciousness in times of danger, when you do not have time to think of solutions, but must simply respond. With training, you will learn to call upon this instinctive part of yourself to help you in any given situation, not just one of immediate danger.

Practical Work

Start the Practical Work for this tree by repeating your basic ritual until you feel a familiarity and understanding of the fir. Then, spend some time in a series of spontaneous Otherworld journeys. Before you start a journey, pick one of your Ogham sticks at random, identify the tree it represents, and base your journey upon the fir and this other tree.

What you are looking to achieve with this exercise is an understanding, at an intuitive level, of how the fir can cause you to say "aah" in surprise and delight with some trees, but in disappointment or even horror with others. Do not shrink away from Otherworld journeys that start to feel uneasy or frightening; you must learn these emotions, understand which tree combinations cause them and why, and then learn to say "aah" in understanding instead.

Start your journey with a fir tree on your right and your other, randomly chosen tree on your left. Call to mind exactly what these two trees represent, especially on an emotional level, and look to see if these sets of emotions manifest in your daily life. Once you have a rough idea of what this entails, walk along a path lined on one side by tall firs, and on the other by the second tree. Eventually, this long avenue will open up to reveal a scene, which could be a forest clearing, a village, a house, or a room—anywhere you might be given the chance to play out the two emotions symbolized by your trees, in a safe, studious environment. Inevitably, other people will be present if you are to attain the maximum benefit from this experience. These people may appear as friends, relatives, work colleagues, or perhaps, famous people. It doesn't matter who they appear to be, don't place too much emphasis on this; they are only symbolic of the energies and character types needed for you to have a full emotional experience. Whoever they are, and whatever they do, put as much into your part as you can. These scenes are absolutely real, even though they do not have a physical presence. You can and will learn from them, but only if you treat them as reality.

It is crucial that you close down these Otherworld journeys slowly and completely. They will not all be of earth shattering importance, but some of them may be upsetting and hard to handle. It is never a good idea to bring to your daily consciousness emotions that have been created during one of these journeys. Closing correctly is more important now than ever before. You may wish to devise a formal, physically involved way of doing this.

You do not need to go through such a journey with the fir and all of the other trees studied so far. Try three or four, and note how they differ. Record all your experiences carefully and in as much detail as possible in your magical diary. The next four Practical Work exercises repeat this basic principle, substituting each of the other four vowels for the fir. By the end of this series of Otherworld experiences, you will have a large body of knowledge to call upon. Your tree vocabulary is getting bigger all the time.

CHAPTER TWENTY-ONE

FURZE

Name: Onn
Letter: O
Ogham letter: ╫
Textual reference: Onn that is Furze.
Word Ogham of Morainn: CONGNAID ECH,
helper of horses, ONNAID equals wheels of a
chariot. ALITER COMGUINIDECH, equally
wounding. Whin.
Word Ogham of Cuchulain: LUTH FIANN .i.
FRAECH, strength of warriors, fierceness.
Word Ogham of Aonghus: FOILLEM SAIRE,
gentlest of work.

Physical Level

I mentioned the furze, or gorse as it is more commonly known, when we examined the letter *nGetal*, the broom. The gorse has very few medicinal properties. A decoction can be made of the flowers that appear throughout the year, which is particularly effective against jaundice and helps to cleanse the kidneys of stones and obstructions. Its wood burns fiercely, although gathering and cutting it can be painful, due to its many sharp spines.

It is a prolific plant, and is found all over the British Isles, especially on open moors and hillsides. In the summer, its bright yellow flowers are a delight to the eye, and the strong scent, which resembles the smell of fresh coconut oil, fills the air with a beautiful perfume. It was at one time cultivated into crude hedges by tenant farmers but, because it spreads so quickly, it was difficult to keep in check. Little or nothing can grow beneath the spreading branches of the bush. It is still a common practice to burn back growth that has become too thick, or which is spreading too far. It is not unusual in rural parts of Britain to see whole hillsides blackened from a recent burning.

Mental Level

The similarities between broom and gorse on a physical level are echoed on the mental level. What has already been said concerning the broom can be applied to the gorse. The references to "horses, chariots, wounding, strength of warriors" and "fierceness" all serve to emphasize a military aspect to the gorse. It has the same aspects of the broom, but on a higher level. Whereas the broom was to be used during a clean-up operation following aborted or abandoned Work, the gorse is to be invoked in cases where resistance is felt from the Work being stopped.

This sounds as if the Work itself—an abstract concept—could take on a vitality and consciousness of its own, and resist being abandoned. This is actually the case, at times, and it is not as odd as it might sound. If you consider that one of the aims of magic is to create that which was not there before, then it is perfectly feasible that you may create an intelligence that was not there before. This does not mean you are acting like a god by creating new life forms, but rather that previously unused life forms, which were already in existence, may take up residence in a mental or spiritual shell or body you have created. If the Work in question is at a stage where it has taken on its own intelligence, it may well decide it does not want to be abandoned, and it may fight your actions to do so. Should this happen, the little broom is not severe enough to over-come this reaction; you must look to the larger and more heavily armed gorse to take over.

It was stressed during our look at the broom that magical hygiene is as important as physical hygiene, and you must always clean up after finishing any magical Workings. Now it is time to realize that one of the effects of any magical Work is that it can bring into an area of your Work an intelligence or consciousness that was not there before. Contrary to mediaeval grimoires, you cannot subjugate these independent intelligences with oaths and threats, nor can you bind them with spells or curses. In nearly every case, you will be Working in perfect harmony with the forces you have invoked, and the idea of abandoning the Work will never come up. In the other Working, when things start to go wrong, or which becomes unnecessary before it is completed, you have a different set of circumstances with which to deal. In such cases, you must be careful you have cleaned up that which is no longer being used, but you must also be able to determine whether or not you have left any half-completed independent intelligences floating about. If you have, or even if you suspect you may have, then the powerful gorse must be invoked to help you complete the mopping up.

The novice magician will not always be in a position to say whether he or she has inadvertently invoked some independent life force requiring the use of the gorse. Should there be any doubt in your mind, always play it safe, and use the gorse anyway. In reality, you probably have little to fear; the novice magician is rarely capable of creating such powerful magic, and magic has its own built-in safeguards. Time, practice, and intuition will tell you when you reach this level of Working.

Spiritual Level

The spiritual exercise for the gorse could be called a moral exercise as well. It raises the question of how you feel about deliberately killing a life force to which you have given an independent consciousness and existence. Does this go against any firmly held beliefs you may have concerning violence and killing? Can you bring yourself to destroy something on one level, which may mean you will be called upon to destroy something on the other levels? You will find yourself in this situation one day, and you must be prepared and know how you are going to react. Listen to your intuition. Give the question some thought on the mental level, but try to set aside any logical arguments for or against such actions for the moment. Your intuition speaks to you in feelings. Your logical mind may tell you that to deliberately kill something is a terrible thing, while at the same time, you may find that you do not *feel* anything wrong with this notion. You must practice paying attention to both, and drawing conclusions from what each has to say.

One conclusion you may come to during such deliberations is that the problem is not whether it is morally right to kill in some circumstances and not others, but whether or not the whole concept of morals actually applies at a spiritual level. You are, ultimately, the only one who can answer this question for yourself. What you have learned about the other trees may help you. Why do you think the Word Ogham of Aonghus refers to the furze as "gentlest of work"? Remember that the word for work can also mean freedom. Why would Aonghus refer to the spiritual meaning of the furze as gentlest of freedom?

Practical Work

Carry out your basic ritual with the furze. As in the last exercise, once you have gained a degree of familiarity, start a series of Otherworld journeys involving the furze and one other tree chosen at random. The scenario for this journey can remain the same as in the last, but the emphasis should be on how the furze can negate the emotion or experience created by the second tree. This negation will take many forms, ranging from extremely direct and violent to extremely subtle and delicate. You may even find yourself in scenes where you take on the role of the furze, and have to carry out the act of destruction yourself. Because of this, the warnings about closing each journey fully and completely apply here, too. You are going to be stirring up some pretty deep, raw, and wild emotions over the next few months. Give yourself an extra few minutes to relax and think over your Otherworld experience before returning to your regular routine.

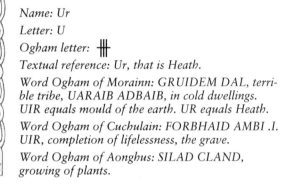

CHAPTER TWENTY-TWO

HEATHER

Name: Ur
Letter: U
Ogham letter: ⵂ
Textual reference: Ur, that is Heath.
Word Ogham of Morainn: GRUIDEM DAL, terrible tribe, UARAIB ADBAIB, in cold dwellings. UIR equals mould of the earth. UR equals Heath.
Word Ogham of Cuchulain: FORBHAID AMBI .I. UIR, completion of lifelessness, the grave.
Word Ogham of Aonghus: SILAD CLAND, growing of plants.

Physical Level

Heather is a twisted and tangled plant which grows in profusion on open moorland, hillsides, and heaths. Its thin stalks are tough and usually longer than they first appear due to the heather's horizontal growth. It bears small purple, red, and bluish flowers which have a delicate aroma and are much favored by bees for their pollen. As a medicinal plant, its uses are mainly in the treatment of nervous complaints and cardiac palpitations. It is not always necessary to actually administer the plant, especially in cases of nervous disorders; as much benefit can be derived simply by walking over a heather-clad moor in the sunshine, enjoying the beautiful sight and inhaling the delicate perfume of the flowers. This

195

experience heightens the senses and spirits, bringing on a calming and soothing effect.

Heather can also help ease the pain of migraine and menstruation. Bees make an excellent honey from its pollen, and the Picts were believed to brew an exceptionally pleasant, but potent, ale from heather. Its tough, twisting roots and stems are still used in the highlands and islands to make ropes, thatch for roofs, and sturdy brooms. It has become quite popular among craftspeople. The many different hues found in the stalks of the different types of heather can be bunched together and polished to produce very colorful and attractive brooches and badges.

The name, Heather, is a popular one for girls in not only Scottish families, but throughout the world. Its Gaelic equivalent, Fraoch, has quite a different meaning, though, and was originally a man's name.

Mental Level

The description of Heather in the Word Ogham of Morainn, "terrible tribe, in cold dwellings, mould of the earth," and in the Word Ogham of Cuchulain, "completion of lifelessness" and "the grave," are all rather bleak and morbid. This implies the heather is a tree connected with death, but the name of the letter in the Tree Ogham, *Ur,* actually means "new" both in Irish and Scottish Gaelic. This apparent contradiction is easily explained by the Celts' unshakable belief in life after death and reincarnation. Dying and being placed in your grave was seen as the first step toward something new. One old Scottish-Gaelic euphemism for death was "the white sleep." This expression was not used because of superstition, or the fear of speaking the words "dead" or "death;" but instead is a kenning to describe the state in which the dead person exists—physically lifeless, but waiting to awaken into the Otherworld. The Word Ogham of Aonghus reflects this notion with the description "growing of plants," which seems to be a complete contradiction of its other descriptions for heather.

The word for heather in Irish and Scottish Gaelic is *fraoch*. This means "fierce" or "war-like," which again gives it a rather different character from the concept of something new. In the Irish legends, there is an important individual called Fraoch who can also be equated with Nechtain, Nuadhu, Conlai, and Neara. His wife was the goddess Boand, and his mother was the warrior-woman Aoife, who also equates with the great warrior-queen Meadhbh of Connacht. His father was the Ulster hero, Cuchulain. All of these family connections give Fraoch a very fierce, warrior-based background. It is recorded in legend that he was killed by his father, and his body was laid in a great cairn. This cairn has been identified with the cave at Cruachan, part of Meadhbh's territory, where an Ogham inscription was found which reads, "*VRACCI MAQVI MEDVVIA*," which means "(the cave of) Fraoch the son of Meadhbh."

If you refer to the letter *Queirt*, you will see that this letter was to be used when "C stands before U," or when *Coll* stands before *Ur*. One meaning of *Coll* is "destruction." When it is combined with *Ur*, you have "destruction preceding something new." Combining this with the other associations of *Ur*—the grave, newness, fierceness, and destruction—the heather clearly represents a phase following violent destruction that heralds the start of something new.

This follows nicely the last tree letter, *Onn* the furze, the true meaning of which is to destroy that which has been created, but which has become unnecessary. We know from the two very diverse sources of ancient Celtic belief and modern science that nothing is ever totally destroyed, it merely changes from one form to another. Therefore, in your clean-up with the furze, what you have destroyed in one form has merely taken on a new existence. The heather is the tree to invoke after all of this cleaning has been completed. You must realize that the last stage of one operation is also the first stage of a new one. Whether you are dealing with physical, mental, or spiritual destruction, you are also, by implication, dealing with physical, mental, or spiritual reconstruction—the perpetual cycle of life, death, and rebirth.

The transition from one state to another can sometimes be unpleasant and very violent. The use of the heather immediately after the use of the furze is to the benefit of the magician in that it can cushion an otherwise overpowering blow. Its use also benefits the life form for the same reason.

Spiritual Level

This renewing property of the heather should help you answer the question posed to you in the last chapter: are you capable of killing and destroying something you have created? You now know that you are not actually killing or destroying anything; you are merely speeding up a change from one state to another, which would happen eventually anyway. This still carries with it a lot of responsibility. It is not all right, for instance, to kill or destroy anything at any time, for any reason, with the justification that you are speeding up evolution. To kill or destroy anything is to take on a tremendous responsibility, and to make yourself totally accountable for the outcome of your actions. You cannot escape this on any level. Under the Irish magical system, you and you alone are responsible for your progress, development, actions, and the consequences of those actions. You must think very carefully about everything you are about to do, and what the outcome is going to be.

Clearly, to take up the furze to destroy something that you have decided is no longer necessary is a very important decision. To have to also consider the likely consequences is weighty indeed. Very often the situation will not be as dramatic it sounds here, but the same principles apply whether you are throwing away a bit of rubbish on the physical level or whether you are performing a powerful ritual on the mental or spiritual levels.

You may notice a distinct difference between this Celtic style of responsibility for your behavior and the teachings of other religions and philosophies. In Celtic magic, you will face the consequences directly, rather than wait for judgment from some higher being. There is no distant retribution or reward, awaiting you in the Otherworld; nor will you pay for your actions in some future incarnation. These concepts of divine reward or retribution as the Christians, Jews, and Moslems know it, or the deeds of one life affecting the next, or Karma as the Hindus know it, are not part of the Celtic system. You are responsible for your actions and their effects and that is it. The Celtic system has a much simpler and, in my opinion, a much fairer outlook on such things.

The lesson for the spiritual level of the heather is to contemplate your personal position in the scheme of things, and ask yourself if you are truly ready to take on the responsibility of destroyer and creator. Remembering that whatever you do to others may eventually be done to you, you must also consider if you are ready to be destroyed at this level and projected into another, unknown level. Think very seriously about the implications of your actions, at all levels, and at all times. Gaining a true understanding of your place in the scheme of things will allow you to exercise your full potential safely. The Practical Work with the heather will help you to resolve some of these issues.

Practical Work

Perform the tree ritual until you are familiar with the heather. Then, as before, link the heather with another tree, and embark on your formal Otherworld journey. It would be a good idea to carry on with the heather from where you left off with the furze, using the same trees you used in the last exercise. This will help you see the consequences of the destruction caused by the furze, and the creation born of that destruction caused by the heather. This exercise will help you experience the ongoing, cyclical nature of creation and destruction.

You should also build into your Practical Work the combination of trees for the double letters involving the heather. In this case, you should be linking with the apple, *Queirt*, the hazel, C, and heather, U. Remember to rotate the linking of the trees through the different combinations of Ogham sticks associated with this these trees (letters).

If you have the inclination, you may use an Otherworld journey to recreate scenes from your own life that initially appeared to be times of death, loss, or destruction, but that now, with the benefit of hindsight, can be seen to have yielded a great deal of positive energy, or even new life.

Try to use this knowledge to see the creation taking place all around you. Use this knowledge to become a conscious creator in this perpetual cycle. The Celtic tradition is unique in world mythologies in that it does not have a Creation Myth explaining how things came into being. The Celts believe that creation is an ongoing process. Working deeply and closely with the heather will help you to understand this better, and to become a player in the game of creation.

CHAPTER TWENTY-THREE

ASPEN

Name: Eadhadh

Letter: E

Ogham letter: ╫╫

Textual reference: Eadhadh (Ed Uath—Horrible grief), Test tree or Aspen.

Word Ogham of Morainn: AERCNAID FER NO FID, distinguished man or wood.

Word Ogham of Cuchulain: BRATHAIR BETHI .i. E, kinsman to the Birch, aspen.

Word Ogham of Aonghus: COMMAIN CARAT, additional name for a friend.

Physical Level

The aspen tree is a distinctive tree with trembling leaves that turn brilliant yellow in autumn. It can grow to sixty-five feet in height, although its trunk appears to stay quite thin for its height. Its leaves are rounded, on alternate sides of the stem, with wavy edges and a flattened stalk. It is this flattened stalk that causes the leaves to tremble even in the slightest breeze. The bark is an attractive silvery-gray with black diamond shapes all over it. Separate trees bear the light-brown male catkins and the green female catkins, which turn white and fluffy in May when they seed.

Like its predecessor in the Tree Ogham, the aspen does not have many medicinal uses. The dried bark, in powdered form, can be mixed with liquid and taken as a treatment for feverish conditions. Its main use is as a means of getting rid of worms and internal parasites in both humans and animals.

Mental Level

The Word Ogham of Morainn, "distinguished man or wood," the Word Ogham of Aonghus, "additional name for a friend," and the Word Ogham of Cuchulain, "kinsman to the birch," do not tell us much about the deeper meanings of the aspen. This is compounded by the fact that the compilers of the *Book of Ballymote* and the other manuscripts seem to have been confused by this tree and letter. It appears with several different spellings: Eadhadh, Eadad, Ebhadh, Ebad, and Eduath; and, in some manuscript listings, it is mixed in with the *forfeda*, the final grouping of double vowels. This could have been a deliberate attempt on the part of the compilers to bury the meaning of the aspen beneath other symbolism, but I doubt it, considering how much they gave away about the other letters and how complicated it would have been to create such a conspiracy. The reason is more likely to have been that even they were unsure about the magical meanings of this tree letter, and perhaps could not agree on it.

To call the aspen "distinguished man or wood" could refer to its physical bark, which is indeed very distinctive. This would be inconsistent with the meanings behind similar textual references for other trees, however, and so must be a deeper association. In fact, the word "distinguished" refers not to the tree, but to the person who has attained this level of progress through experiences with the Tree Ogham. The word for wood, and the word for knowledge, come from the same root in Old Irish. The word "wood" could also be read as "distinguished knowledge." A person having this particular knowledge, gained by self-advancement and deep physical, mental, and spiritual experience, could truly be called distinguished. The mental-level experience of the aspen is an acknowledgment of the successful completion of that which has gone before. The only way, therefore, to achieve this level is to work steadily and progressively through all of the trees, and build the experiences of each one onto the next. The aspen is a sign of achievement or successful attainment.

The aspen was one of the favorite trees of the Irish Celts for making shields. This, coupled with its more esoteric symbolism, is illustrated in the legend of Cuchulain's training in arms on the Isle of Skye. According to this legend, the person who gave the Ulster hero his final training was a woman called Scathach (sky-ah—hence the name of the island). This name means "shadow," but it also means "shield." When the legend opens, it is obvious that Cuchulain was already an expert and proven warrior of this world. The instruction Scathach gave him was not on the physical level, but on the mental or magical level of the Otherworld. From this, it can be deduced that the shield was the symbol of someone who had attained proficiency at all levels. As the shield would most likely have been made of aspen, it can be seen how the tree itself represents achievement and attainment on the magical levels.

Spiritual Level

What has been said of the aspen on the mental level applies equally to the spiritual level. The danger that you must constantly guard against, even at this level of attainment, is falling into the trap of self-importance. You must realize that you are still capable of falling from grace, of making mistakes, and of upsetting the delicate balance of things when you do what you *want* rather than what you *will*. The Word Ogham of Cuchulain expresses this in its association of the aspen as "kinsman to the birch." The birch is the first tree of this magical progression. Cuchulain's words remind you not to forget your humble beginnings.

A greater danger is that the natural safeguards built into magical Workings at the basic levels do not necessarily exist at this level. By now, you should be in full control of the magical forces with which you are Working, and your reasons for using those forces should be in accordance with the Green World laws. The shield is an appropriate symbol for reminding you that your competence does not preclude your needing protection, even at this advanced stage. The shield will protect you from yourself, however, not from other foes. The Word Ogham of Aonghus, "additional name (or synonym) for a friend," sums up your relationship with the aspen.

One reason why the safeguards built into the lower levels have been removed at this stage is that you have attained a degree of proficiency that requires experimentation for further progress. You must think out new combinations of trees to Work with, new forces to invoke, and look for new ground to be broken for the benefit of those yet to come. This is what happens in the academic world, where the doctor or professor learns as much as he or she can, then goes into research to come up with new theories, practices, and knowledge to pass on to students still working through the lower grades. If the safeguards of these lower grades were not removed during such experimental and pioneering work, the restrictions they impose would prohibit advances and discoveries from being made at all.

A great deal of damage can be done by those Working recklessly at this level, but the spiritual-level lesson of the aspen is to be aware of this responsibility and the power you have on all levels, and to be sure that you are capable of controlling that power. It also means you must be prepared to take calculated risks. The experimental aspect of the aspen is suggested in its other name of "Test tree." There is a passage in the "Cattle Raid of Cooley" that warns of what can happen if a magician or warrior goes against the laws of magic and the Green World when insufficiently qualified to cope with the effects of such action. In this passage, Cuchulain has upset three brothers, Lon, Ualu, and Diliu, and they have decided to ambush and kill him. Knowing that he is a dangerous adversary, they enlist the help of their three charioteers, Meslir, Meslaech, and Meslethan. This went against the rules of Celtic warfare. Charioteers were not allowed to take an active part in combat and, consequently, warriors were not allowed to attack charioteers.

> Three shafts of aspen were cut for their charioteers, so
> that all six could go against him together, thus breaking
> the rules of fair fight. But he slew them all.[1]

The message is quite clear: Experiment, yes, but stick to the rules. Your Practical Work with the aspen should help you to better understand this.

Practical Work

Carry out your tree ritual as you have been, and build a good knowledge of and relationship with the aspen. Once you have achieved this, start a series of Otherworld journeys linking the aspen to other randomly chosen trees. What happens after that is entirely up to you. The main way to progress with the aspen is to experiment; but you must devise your own experiments and research to learn what you need to know. I cannot tell you what to do. I would suggest that this experimentation take a structured form, and be based on areas where you need more answers. These areas should already be clear to you after the extensive work you have completed. Use this time fruitfully. Use your knowledge to gain more knowledge. You have learned the language of the trees, and can now read and write as you will. What a very exciting time!

---

[1] Cecile O'Rahilly, *Tain Bo Cuailgne* (Dublin: Irish Texts Society, 1962).

CHAPTER TWENTY-FOUR

YEW

Name: Idhadh
Letter: I
Ogham letter: 卌
Textual reference: Ido, Yew.
Word Ogham of Morainn: SINEM FEDHA, oldest
of woods. IBUR equals service tree, Yew.
Word Ogham of Cuchulain: LUTH (NO LITH)
LOBAIR .i. AES, strength (or color) of a sick man,
people or an age.
Word Ogham of Aonghus: CAINED SEN NO
AILEAM AIS, abuse for an ancestor or pleasing
consent.

Physical Level

The yew lives the longest of all the trees we have
examined. Until very recently, it was believed that
the maximum age for these trees was about eight
hundred years, but research work by dendrochro-
nologists is now beginning to indicate that some
yew trees in British churchyards may be as much as
four thousand years old. This far exceeds the life
span of the American Giant Redwoods and
Bristlecone Pines, which have been considered the
oldest trees on the planet. The fact that most of
these ancient British yews are in churchyards indicates that the church buildings were deliberately
situated next to what would have already been an
ancient tree. Perhaps the reverence for this tree was

continued by the newly converted Christians, who had held it in great respect in their pre-Christian days. Despite its great age, it is not the tallest of trees, growing to an average height of only fifty feet. What it lacks in stature, it makes up for in girth, spreading itself widely and often developing several substantial trunks from the same roots.

The yew is an evergreen, and has dark green needles that are light on the underside, and that sit on alternate sides of the green stems. It bears a bright, red fruit that contains a single seed. The female flowers are green and very small, whereas the male flowers, which appear on different trees, are slightly larger and yellow in color. The bark is smooth, light brown, and very flaky. The wood is orange-brown and has a very attractive grain. It was much favored in mediaeval times for making longbows, and was harvested to such an extent that the tree's existence became threatened. It is now more abundant than ever, and is no longer in danger. Its suitability for use as a bow was known long before mediaeval or even Celtic times, as evidenced by the almost perfectly preserved body of a StoneAge hunter found in 1991 in the Alps. Among his belongings was a bow made of yew.

The needles, bark, sap, and seeds are all extremely poisonous and have no medicinal uses whatsoever. Should you need to handle living or dead yew trees, branches, or needles, wear protective gloves and wash your hands thoroughly as soon as possible afterwards. Recent work by doctors and scientists in America has produced a solution called "Taxol," made from the bark of the yew. This formula has been used successfully in the treatment of certain cancers, but this type of medicinal work is clearly beyond the scope of the average student of the trees, and I would again warn you not to experiment with the yew as a medicinal tree.

The name MacIvor, or MacIver, may come from the Gaelic meaning "Son of the Yew." The small village of Dunure, in Ayrshire, Scotland, derives its name from an old Gaelic title meaning "Fort of the Yew." Some writers claim this village, with its tiny, ruined castle, has an Arthurian connection, and may be the original Camelot. Certainly its close proximity to the Isle of Arran, which was the original Avalon, gives this theory some weight.

Mental Level

The Word Ogham of Morainn's references to the yew tree as the "oldest of woods" and "Ido—the yew," are simple statements of fact that tell us nothing deeper. Paradoxically, this tells us more about the yew than the textual references have said about any of the other trees. This is because the yew represents the sum total of all that has gone before it. The yew simply is, and that is all there is to it. It is the longest-living tree in the Tree Ogham, it is an evergreen, and it is the only poisonous tree. This poisonous aspect on the physical level applies equally on the other levels. If you abuse the yew physically, you will be poisoned physically. If you abuse it mentally—for example, by trying to claim you know more than it can tell you—you are likely to poison yourself mentally. The result of this will be like the tragic person whose ego has gone totally out of control. Unfortunately, in the world of magic, this seems to happen quite frequently.

The only thing that needs to be said about the mental level of the yew is that it exists, and you need do nothing about it. If you have achieved the magical power and the true ability to understand and use it wisely, as symbolized by the aspen, then all you need to be aware of is that the yew tree stands next in line to sum up the other trees that have preceded it.

The old word for the yew, *Eo*, is also an old word for "salmon." In Celtic lore, the salmon was believed to contain the sum of all knowledge within its body. Eating of the Salmon of Knowledge gave the diner the answers to everything he or she ever needed to know. Such is the experience of the yew. This might imply, to some people, that there is a shortcut through the forest of the Tree Ogham. It could be misinterpreted as meaning that, by studying the yew to gain knowledge of the other trees instead of going through the lengthy and laborious study of them individually, you will reach the same ends more quickly. It does not work like that; and the yew's poisonous aspect serves as a warning. There are no shortcuts in magic. In the Word Ogham of Aonghus's curious description of the yew as "abuse for an ancestor" or "pleasing consent," you can see that if you try to take shortcuts, you will certainly abuse your ancestors, whom you should hold in great respect. If, however, you tread the same, long, slow path they did, you will gain their pleasing consent and assistance in the Otherworld.

Spiritual Level

The yew was the most revered of all trees by the Irish druids. It was used by them in the preparation of magical wands and in divination, but these druids had undergone an extremely arduous training before they were permitted to do these dangerous deeds. It is unlikely that any of us will ever achieve the same proficiency as they did. The spiritual lesson of the yew is the same as the physical and mental, which is that it is, and that is all you need to know. It is foolish and dangerous to tamper with the yew on a spiritual level.

The importance of the yew is highlighted by its inclusion as two of the Five Great Trees of Ireland. It is believed that these specific trees were used as gathering sites for both armies and druids, and it is clearly no accident that yews were chosen.

The further along the Tree Ogham you go, the less can be said about each tree, and the fewer uses each seems to have. The yew is the final example of this, where to all intents and purposes, it has no uses at all, and nothing can be said about it. This is the state we are in when we first enter this world. Our potential is infinite. Just as the yew contains all the properties, uses, and symbolism of all the trees that have gone before, so do we, at birth, contain the experiences, knowledge, and understanding of our ancestors. One technique of magic is to identify that knowledge, and to identify the tools and methods needed to unlock it. If you have truly reached the level of the yew, then it is time to go back to the beginning, to the humble birch, and start again.

A reference to yew in one of the *Lays of Fionn*, known as the "Lament for the Fianna," seems to imply that the mighty warrior band had come to an end:

> A prophecy that Fionn made, on Samhain's Eve in the Yew Glen, that the faultless Fianna should depart, and that it should be an end of us tonight. Tonight it is an utter end.[1]

The yew had come into play, and all that could be experienced had been experienced. All appeared to be at an end. The fact that this utterance was made on Samhain's Eve, and in a glen of yew trees, shows that everything had been experienced and completed on one level, and now would rise to the next. Samhain is the start of the Celtic new year, a beginning if ever there was one. The yew represents the final stage of one level of learning but, more importantly, the beginning stage of the next level.

Practical Work

Examine your relationship to the yew, and your understanding of it as a tree, by carrying out the basic ritual. Once you have achieved this, take a look at the way the previous five trees relate to each other by using the visualization suggested earlier. Go on to introduce the previous ten trees, fifteen trees, and finally, all of the

---

[1] Gerard Murphy, trans., *Duanaire Finn*, (Dublin: Irish Texts Society, 1933).

consonant and vowel trees together. A complete forest of twenty trees will now be open to you to enter and explore.

This will take a long time to complete, but you must fully understand all the trees to speak the language of the trees fluently. The last stage in this Practical Work is to go back to the very beginning of the Tree Ogham, to the birch, and start again. This time, look at the trees in more depth and with a deeper understanding of how they relate one to the other in the set order of the *Beithe Luis Nion*. You may decide to step sideways, as it were, and instead of going through all of the trees again, start a study of the other forms of Ogham, perhaps Bird Ogham or Color Ogham. Using a new set of correspondences and symbols may be a good idea, as it keeps the Practical Work fresh. The choice is yours.

In Part Three, I give some examples of how to start interpreting the multiple-tree passages found in the legends. I also introduce a slight change to the basic ritual to help you further your understanding of each tree, your special relationship with it, and your use of these concepts in your day-to-day and magical lives.

PART
THREE

CHAPTER TWENTY-FIVE

COMBINATIONS OF TREES

If you have managed to follow the path through the forest of the Tree Ogham, you have realized by now that there is a lot of important lore in there, and that it will take a long time to sort it all out. Persistent and patient Work with the trees will pay off, and enough information has been provided so far for you to form your own theories about tree Working. This, combined with a study of the trees themselves, should help you to develop your own system of tree correspondences and uses. This is not the whole picture, however. Tree magic is only one aspect of the Celtic magical tradition. You must learn how this form of magical Working fits into the entire scheme of things. You must understand where our knowledge of the Celtic tree magic system comes from, and how this information has been passed on for so many generations.

The main source of knowledge is the huge body of Irish Celtic legends. By reading between the lines of these fantastic stories, and by recognizing the symbolism employed in the outer narrative, you will find the keys to unlock the magical instruction contained therein.

The importance of trees, on a magical level, is expressed time and time again in these legends, where a tree crops up in a story and we are told exactly which species of tree it is. The legends rarely make vague statements such as "They met by a tree," or "She sheltered under a large tree"; they are much more specific, for example, "They met by a rowan tree" or "She sheltered under a large yew tree." This naming of trees is deliberate, and if you keep in mind the magical meanings, uses, and symbolism of the trees, you will realize just how much information these ancient legends convey. You will also find that even obscure passages will suddenly become clear and relevant to you when the time is right.

For this reason, you should not dismiss passages that do not make sense to you at first. They may contain information or instruction that you do not need now, but may need later. This will show real progress when you open your magical intuition and awareness, and things that had previously been obscure become clear and comprehensible. As you change while you learn and progress, so will the legends change. They will reveal part of their inner meaning at one time, and another part at another time, and only when you are ready for that knowledge.

As far as we are concerned in this present study, the important parts of the legends are the sections that refer to more than one tree at the same time or in the same incident. These multiple-tree passages can be difficult to interpret on a magical level, especially when you consider how abstract and multi-faceted some of the trees are. Those of you with an interest in code-breaking should find this whole concept challenging, for this is essentially what we shall be doing. Each tree is a symbol or cipher. When these individual symbols are placed in conjunction with others in a specific order, the combined meaning of their individual symbols takes on a much deeper and much more instructive character.

Children learning the alphabet and rules of spelling and grammar are often introduced to simple songs and rhymes designed to develop their memory, giving them practical examples of the use of words. In a similar fashion, we will start our examination of the combined effects of the trees by looking at a simple song. This is an Old English folk song, which contains some very straightforward, practical advice on which types of wood are good for burning, and which are best to avoid.

Oak logs will warm you well,

That are old and dry;

Logs of pine will sweetly smell

But the sparks will fly.

Birch logs will burn too fast,

Chestnut scarce at all;

Hawthorn logs are good to last—

Cut them in the fall.

Holly logs will burn like wax,

You may burn them green;

Elm logs like to smoldering flax,

No flame to be seen.

Beech logs for winter time,

Yew logs as well;

Green elder logs it is a crime

For any man to sell.

Pear logs and apple logs,

They will scent your room,

Cherry logs across the dogs

Smell like flower of broom.

Ash logs smooth and gray,

Burn them green or old,

Buy up all that come your way—

Worth their weight in gold.[1]

It may be that there was some deeper meaning to this song originally but, if there was, it has been lost to us today and we are left with only the physical-level aspect. It contains references to trees that do not appear in the Tree Ogham and that were introduced into Britain long after the Tree Ogham had been formulated, and this may indicate a late date for its composition. Nonetheless, this song has a very similar feel and content to a passage from an old Irish legend. It could be that it is a corrupted folk memory of the instructions contained within the older Irish version, the deeper meanings of which had been forgotten.

This Irish legend is known as *Aided Fergusa meic Leide*, the "Death of Fearghus mac Leide," and centers on the activities of

---

[1] *The Woodcutter's Song* words traditional English with additional lyrics by Robin Williamson, music by Robin Williamson and Chris Caswell. The album *A Glint at the Kindling* was released in 1992 on the TMC label, catalog number TMC 9201. See the Discography for details on how to obtain Robin's works.

Iubhdan (yoo-dan), the King of the Leprechauns. Iubhdan travels to the court of the King of Ulster to see for himself if there really are people bigger, stronger, and braver than Leprechauns. Superficially, this legend is a comedy, full of bizarre characters and incidents that seem to have little meaning; but, as is often the case with such apparently ridiculous tales, it contains different layers of interpretation and quite a few well-disguised references to initiations and progression along a magical path.

Iubhdan gives out various bits of advice and instruction throughout the legend. One which will concern us appears to be no more than a list of which woods are good for burning and which to avoid, like the song quoted above. As we shall see, however, it has a much deeper aspect to it. It is a good example of how trees are sometimes used in legends to give sound magical advice to those who have the knowledge to understand. This section centers on a man called Fear Diadh (fahr djaya), Man of Smoke, who is lighting a fire and throwing onto it various kinds of wood. Iubhdan is horrified by the man's obvious ignorance and reckless handling of the different woods. He says the following words to Fear Diadh:

> O man that for Fearghus of the feasts dost kindle fire, whether afloat or ashore never burn the king of woods. Monarch of Innisfail's forests the woodbine is, whom none may hold captive; no feeble sovereign's effort it is to hug all tough trees in his embrace. The pliant woodbine, if thou burn, wailings for misfortune will abound; dire extremity at weapons' points or drowning in great waves will come after. Burn not the precious apple tree of spreading and low sweeping bough of white, against whose fair head all men put forth the hand. The surly blackthorn is a wanderer, and a wood that the artificer burns not; throughout his body, though it be scanty, birds in their flocks warble. The noble willow burn not, a tree sacred to poems; within his bloom bees are a-sucking, all

love the little cage. The graceful tree with the berries, the wizard's tree, the rowan, burn; but spare the limber tree: burn not the slender hazel. Dark is the color of the ash: timber that makes the wheels to go; rods he furnishes for horse-men's hands, and his form turns the battle into flight. Tenterhook among woods the spiteful briar is, by all means burn him that is so keen and green; he cuts, he flays the foot, and him that would advance he forcibly drags backward. Fiercest heat-giver of all is green oak, from him none may escape unhurt: by partiality for him the head is set on aching and by his acrid embers the eye is made sore. Alder, very battle-witch of all woods, tree that is hottest in the fight—undoubtingly burn at thy discretion both the alder and the whitethorn. Holly, burn it green; holly, burn it dry: of all trees whatsoever the critically best is holly. Elder that hath tough bark, tree that in truth hurts sore: him that furnishes horses to the armies from the Sidhe burn so that he be charred. The birch as well, if he be laid low, promises abiding fortune: burn up most sure and certainly the stalks that bear the constant pods. Suffer, if it so please thee, the russet aspen to come headlong down: burn, be it late or early, the tree with the palsied branch. Patriarch of long lasting woods is the yew, sacred to feasts as is well known: of him now build ye dark red vats of goodly size. Fear Diadh, thou faithful one, wouldst thou but do my behest: to thy soul as to thy body, O man, 'twould work advantage![2]

There is a similarity between the sentiments of this passage and the information contained in the folk song given above, but you can see there is a lot more to this than meets the eye. If we look at Iubhdan's comments concerning the various trees in a bit more

---

[2] S.H. O'Grady, *Silva Gadelica*, Vol. 2 (Dublin: Williams & Norgate, 1892).

detail, we will be able to confirm what was said earlier about the nature, purposes, and Otherworld symbolic meanings of the trees as given in the Tree Ogham. The trees have been set out in a specific sequence to convey a definite meaning and series of instructions to the knowledgeable listener.

The trees mentioned by Iubhdan, and the order in which they appear, are woodbine, apple, blackthorn, willow, rowan, hazel, ash, briar, oak, alder, whitethorn, holly, elder, birch, aspen, and yew. All of these trees are named in the Tree Ogham, but note that the vine, broom, fir, and heather are missing. The first tree mentioned by Iubhdan is the woodbine, which he calls the "Monarch of Innisfail's forests." Innisfail literally means "Island of Destiny," and is an old poetic name for Ireland. It is clear Iubhdan considers the woodbine to be the most powerful of trees, for not only is it the first tree mentioned, it is also the one with the longest reference. If you consider that the woodbine and the ivy are interchangeable, you will see that this is exactly what was said during our study of the ivy in Chapter Sixteen. The ivy/woodbine is the most powerful of trees because it can unite all other trees, and it can kill them. Iubhdan's description, "no feeble sovereign's effort it is to hug all tough trees in his embrace," suggest the action of the ivy. You should almost never consciously use the ivy in magical Working. It is a tree that the guides in the Otherworld may use to warn you that you are going in the wrong direction. This is how it is used in the above passage. Iubhdan, a Leprechaun, or man from the Otherworld, is attempting to warn Fear Diadh, a man of this world, that he is on the wrong track, and that he must stop and take corrective action. A deeper knowledge of the woodbine would put him in a better position to understand the rest of the trees. Iubhdan's statement "...whether afloat or ashore never burn the king of woods" would not seem to be referring to the physical level (how can you burn wood while afloat?). Being afloat or ashore is a kenning for being in the Otherworld or being in this world. In other words, this is not a tree to be tampered with in either world. Iubhdan's warning is fierce:

221

"wailings for misfortune will abound; dire extremity at weapons' points or drowning in great waves will come after."

The legends of the Otherworld often describe it as being reached by boat. This opening tree is saying that Fear Diadh has started something inadvisable, and he will have to travel to the Otherworld to learn the corrective action to take. Some of this information will be given to him in the rest of Iubhdan's instructions.

The next tree named is the apple, which shifts everything to the Otherworld point of view. The apple is both a powerful symbol for Otherworld voyagers, and a useful tool once there. The Word Ogham of Morainn makes much of the apple's sheltering qualities, and this is what Iubhdan is referring to when he describes its "spreading and low-sweeping branches." This should be read symbolically, as apple trees do not have spreading or low-sweeping branches. "Against whose fair head all men put forth the hand" is a reference to the silver apple branch as a symbol of the Otherworld when used by those of the Otherworld voyaging to this world or by those of this world voyaging to the Otherworld. This is the excellent emblem, a sign of protection, which Cuchulain describes in his Word Ogham.

Note that the apple is described as a "tree ever decked in bloom of white" which, of course, it is not. In this world, it is only in bloom during the spring and early summer; but it is permanently in bloom in the Otherworld. Iubhdan's instruction to Fear Diadh is to take up the sheltering emblem of the apple branch, and go forth into the Otherworld.

The blackthorn is a continuation of the message of the apple tree. Both are associated with moving from this world to the Otherworld, and both are associated with sheltering and with shamen. The tree in which "birds in their flocks warble" can be read on a physical level, as many species of birds do prefer this tree for nesting. The reference to birds can also be read on a higher level, as a reference to the shaman, the voyager between the worlds, in his or her cloak of bird-feathers. The flowers of the blackthorn are white with red tips, and are very symbolic of the Otherworld. Otherworld animals, such as cows and dogs, are always described in the legends as having white skin and red ears. Iubhdan describes the blackthorn as a "wanderer." This can be read on two levels. Physically, this may refer to the fact that it spreads itself in all directions, rather than simply growing straight up in the air as most trees do. On a higher level of meaning, we know that this tree represents the transition from this world to the Otherworld. Its main symbolic function is for the magician to think over his own death, and this is what is being told to Fear Diadh. As with the previous two trees, Fear Diadh is urged not to burn the blackthorn.

The willow is described by Iubhdan as a "little cage." This could be a reference to the fact that willow rods were used in the construction of boxes, baskets, and small cages. Its Otherworld significance, however, is echoed by Iubhdan when he says, "a tree sacred to poems; within his bloom bees are a-sucking." Both poems and bees were believed to have Otherworld connections. Iubhdan is telling Fear Diadh that, once he has progressed through the blackthorn stage, he must be prepared to raise his consciousness a level—one of the symbolic meanings of the willow. He must also give up any ties which still bind him to this world—another of the meanings of the willow.

The rowan is also strongly connected with the Otherworld and with magic. Iubhdan's name for the rowan is "the wizard's tree." It is the first tree that he tells Fear Diadh to burn. To us of this world, such an action would be considered extremely unlucky. This reversal of what is lucky and unlucky is due to the fact that these words are coming from an Otherworld character, and things tend to be reversed from that perspective. It reflects the need for acceptance of both sides of things, the good and the bad, as discussed in Chapter Six.

At this high Otherworld level the apparent differences between what is good and what is bad do not exist. The fact that this is the first tree Fear Diadh is told to burn is also significant. It indicates that it is the first tree to be used in a positive way. The instructions Iubhdan has been giving to Fear Diadh got him to the highest level of the Otherworld, from which he can take positive action with his own magical powers. The Work has begun!

Hazel, despite its importance in the Tree Ogham, is hardly mentioned in this tree poem. Quite honestly, there is no reason why each and every tree has to be given a lengthy discourse. Note, for example, the vine, broom, fir, and heather are not even cited. The hazel is an indication to look for knowledge, which is what the nature of Fear Diadh's Otherworld magical Work should be. In this context, merely mentioning a tree is enough to convey this meaning.

Ash is strongly connected with the breaking of peace, and with deliberately going forward to face new challenges. This is put poetically by Iubhdan when he says, "timber that makes the wheels to go; rods he furnishes for horsemen's hands." It is known that ash wood was used in the construction of horse-drawn chariots, and horsemen's goads may have been made of the strong, straight ash. The deeper meaning, the will of the magician, suggests that it is time to take up the Spear or Wand and start the practical magical Work. There is a hint at the beginning of the description of the ash that may indicate this Work could be somber or depressing. Iubhdan says, "Dark is the color of the ash." This cannot refer to the physical tree, which has light-colored bark and very white wood. Iubhdan must be referring to its inner meaning, which is not going to be so clear and bright.

The briar, or furze, is the next tree mentioned in the poem, and its descriptions appear more or less as simple statements of fact. "Burn him that is so keen and green," and "he flays the foot" refers to the ease of burning and many sharp spines of the briar; and "him that would advance he forcibly drags backwards," refers to how important it is to clean up after one magical operation before advancing to the next. Iubhdan is advising Fear Diadh to follow up his creative activity with the cleansing effects of the furze. One is clearly linked to the other in this particular sequence.

Note the strong command "by all means burn him." Whenever you get such a strong direction to burn a tree, which on the physical level means to release its energy, you should read this as a kenning telling you to use the tree positively and forcefully on a higher level.

The oak's descriptions, "fiercest heat giver of all...from him none may escape unhurt...the head is set on aching...the eye is made sore," seem to infer that this tree symbolizes the culmination of the whole Working, and that it is at this stage the full effects are going to be felt. These are also references to the oak's warrior connections, which carry on the martial aspects introduced by the ash/Spear and the furze/killing or destroying aspect. This tree symbolizes completion, but also the very real need to keep yourself anchored firmly in the physical world, where you live out the greatest part of your physical incarnation, and to learn and progress from your experiences so far. This suggests that Iubhdan is telling Fear Diadh that his Work is now completed but, because the poem goes on for a few more lines, this is clearly not the case.

The references to the "green oak," "the head is set on aching," and "the eye is made sore," are all references to the Lord of the Hunt—the Green Man—who is associated with the Green World in the form of the oak tree. He had one eye, and was in the habit of hitting people over the head with his massive iron club. On a purely physical level, these references could be to the effects of inhaling the acrid smoke caused by burning green oak. As always, there are several layers of meaning to these cryptic statements. The connections between the oak and the next two trees, the alder and the whitethorn, are made by the statement that these three are all good burners. The martial theme is similarly carried on with the alder, described as "very battle-witch of all woods, tree that is hottest in the fight." This is a reference to the shield made of alder, used by the warrior during military campaigns. This is a warning to Fear Diadh to watch out for a continuing reaction to his earlier magical Work, despite the fact that he has already passed the completion stage—

the oak. He must be prepared to defend himself against something yet to come, which is symbolized by the whitethorn or hawthorn.

To "undoubtingly burn" the whitethorn could be a reference to its overtly horrible aspect, but this is subtly muted by the phrase, "at thy discretion." Discrimination and discretion are the two most important virtues a magician must exercise. This, and the protective nature of the alder, seem to be telling Fear Diadh to have the courage of his magical convictions, to go forward under the protection of the alder shield, and face up to the horrors or terrors of the hawthorn, which he has incurred due to the earlier magical Working being so powerful and so successful. By facing the unpleasant side-effects of his Working, he will negate them, or burn them out, and be able to move on to the next important stage of this complicated set of instructions.

The next tree named is holly. Its triple aspect is presented here when the name of the tree is given three times. "Burn it green, burn it dry" refers to its reincarnation aspects, and to the fact that it symbolizes the continuation of life, the change from one state to another, or to put it simply, progress. It is appropriate that this should be brought into the poem immediately after Fear Diadh has been encouraged to go forth into battle and face up to some horror or other. Iubhdan is indicating that things are still going according to plan, and will continue to do so. The kenning for progress and releasing energy—burning wood—is used very forcibly here when Iubhdan says, "of all the trees whatsoever the critically best is holly." On the physical level, holly would not normally be regarded as the best wood for burning.

The elder tree is the tree "that in truth hurts sore." This is the tree that forces you to face up to painful realizations. You must have "tough bark" to accept these truths about yourself. This continues the lesson of the holly given immediately before. The text then says, "burn so that he be charred," which tells you not to destroy it completely, but only burn away the bits that are not needed. The elder's Otherworld connections are strongly emphasized here by the reference to the Sidhe, the fairy host.

Next, Fear Diadh is told that the birch "if he be laid low promises abiding fortune." This refers to its self-sacrificing aspect. Its reincarnation powers are then referred to by "burn up most sure and certainly the stalks that bear the constant pods," a timely piece of reassurance for poor old Fear Diadh, who by now must be either completely baffled by Iubhdan's rantings or completely terrified by them.

Finally, Iubhdan introduces the aspen and the yew at the end of the poem. These symbolize the completion of the Work. It will be noted that they are given in the same order in this poem as they are in the Tree Ogham, where they also symbolize completion and attainment. Aspen receives a very brief, matter-of-fact mention, which indicates that it is not to be actively invoked during this particular magical formula, but, coupled with the yew, it shows that Iubhdan has given out all the instruction he can to Fear Diadh. Now that he has reached this stage, he can reflect upon his achievements. Fear Diadh is not told to burn the yew, but to "build ye dark-red vats of goodly size," and that it is "sacred to feasts." Now the magical Working contained within Iubhdan's lengthy formula is complete, and it is time to celebrate.

We can sum up this series of instructions from Iubhdan to Fear Diadh by saying: You are doing something wrong (woodbine), and you must go to the Otherworld bearing the recognized symbol of your office and powers (apple) to correct this error. You must do this by using your shamanic powers to let go totally of this world (blackthorn), and rise to the highest level in the Otherworld (willow). Start to use your magical skills at this level, but note that polarities may be reversed (rowan). Look for the knowledge or inspiration that you will need to help you complete the Work in hand (hazel). Once you have found this, go ahead, using your Spear or Wand (ash) to produce the changes which are the purpose behind this journey to the Otherworld. Part of this operation will involve the cleaning up of something which has been left unfinished (briar). This will require a great deal of effort, magical power, and a certain amount of danger in its completion (oak, alder, and hawthorn). Once this has been completed, realize that things will best progress (holly) by doing away with the parts of your personality that are no longer needed (elder). This painful process is a necessary form of self-sacrifice (birch). After all this has been successfully completed, realize the good that has been done by your efforts (aspen). Finally, acknowledge the completion of this important magical Working (yew).[3]

Once all this symbolic instruction has been given, Iubhdan's final words to Fear Diadh are:

> Fear Diadh, thou faithful one, wouldst thou but do my behest: to thy soul as to thy body, O man, 'twould work advantage![4]

This comparison of the soul with the body, the spiritual with the physical, is the hub of the Irish Celtic magical system. The spiritual and the physical are inextricably linked, and successful magic on one level will manifest equally successfully on the others; even the King of the Leprechauns knows that.

---

[3] This is my interpretation of the passage. You may find that you come up with a different interpretation, based upon your own realizations and Work with trees. Trees change shape, size, width, color, and every other aspect of their physical appearance as they grow and progress. So, too, do their inner meanings change in relation to the person studying them. Read my explanation to start to understand the principle of interpreting the trees on a higher level. Once you have grasped this principle, then try to come to your own understanding of these passages from Celtic legends.

[4] O'Grady.

Practical Work

The next step in your Practical Work is to once again go through all of the trees in order, but this time the emphasis will be on understanding their relationship to the Four Elements, Earth, Water, Fire, and Air, the building blocks of the universe.

Open your circle as before, spending a few moments stilling your mind and slowing down your thought processes. Once you feel ready, take your Stone from its position on the perimeter of your circle, and sit at the foot of your tree with the Stone on your lap, facing the Northern quarter. Think about all the symbolism connected with the North, and its connections with the Element of Earth. Consider the way in which your tree is composed of earth. Think of the wonderful process it has gone through, from sending out its first tiny shoots into the soil when it was a mere seed or nut, and how those tiny shoots have grown and developed into the strong, deep-reaching lifelines that continue to suck up the earth and form it into the tree that now is supporting your back. This is truly a remarkable process, and is exactly the same as the one which gave rise to you, and to the body you now inhabit. The only difference is that you are mobile and can go in search of food, whereas the tree is static and must depend on one patch of earth to sustain it.

Try to consider and understand how the tree views this relationship with the Element of Earth. Look to your own relationship with the land and the Element of Earth. Can you see similarities between your perceptions and those of the tree? Repeat the process on different occasions, with your Wand and the Element of Fire in the South. Think of how the heat of the sun, and the internal heat of the earth and the tree, all combine to help the tree grow and maintain its health. Compare this to your own relationship to the Element of Fire.

Carry out the exercise again in the East, with your Knife and the Element of Air. Think about your relationship with Air, and also the tree's very special relationship with this most important of Elements. Trees breathe out oxygen as a gift of life to all other living creatures. Do you take this for granted, or can you begin to see just how dependent on trees we really are?

Finally, take a look at the Western quarter with your Cup and the Element of Water. Consider how tree roots suck up water and allow it to flow through the whole of the tree, just like the blood in human veins. Consider how tree roots can change the flow of underground water, and consequently the physical appearance of the land. Establish a deep understanding of the tree's relationship to these Elements, and complement this with a deeper understanding of your own fragile relationship with them.

Do not forget to formally close down your Practical Work by first thanking the tree for its help and cooperation, then replacing whatever Magical Weapon you have been Working with at its appropriate quarter before redrawing the circle in reverse and removing your Magical Weapons. Remember to write a full account of your actions and realizations in your magical diary.

It could be very painful to sit with your back against a hawthorn tree or furze bush. Similarly, it will be impossible to sit against a broom, vine, or even ivy. In these cases, it is acceptable to sit within your circle, at the appropriate quarter, and hold a twig, leaf, or branch of the relevant tree in your lap with your Magical Weapon.

CHAPTER TWENTY-SIX

THE FRENZY OF MAD SWEENEY

Of all the Irish legends that contain magical tree references, the longest and most informative must surely be the legend known as *Buile Suibhne Geilt*, the "Frenzy of Mad Sweeney." It is difficult to say when this complex combination of prose and poetry was first composed, but based on a linguistic analysis of the text, it was probably first written down around the year 1200. The written version would have been based on a much older oral tradition, the date of which is impossible to establish. A historical reference is made in the text to the Battle of Magh Rath, which was fought in the year 637. It may be the case that the central character, Suibhne (Sweeney), is based upon an actual person mentioned in other legends as well as in some of the historical annals.

Caution is called for when trying to establish the identities of characters from the legends and annals. Suibhne was a common name, and there are many Suibhnes mentioned in legends. Keep in mind during this study that whether or not Suibhne actually existed is irrelevant. What is important to us is what he is attributed with saying.

The story of Suibhne is as follows: Suibhne, who is naked at the time, attacks St. Ronan, who is trying to build a church in his territory of Dal Araidhe. In his anger, Suibhne throws the saint's Psalter into a lake, just as a messenger arrives from the king of Ulster, asking him to help at the battle of Magh Rath. Suibhne leaves to go to battle, and St. Ronan curses him that he should be driven mad and spend the rest of his days wandering the woods naked until he is finally killed by a spear on the very day that he next sets eyes on the saint's Psalter (which had by now been restored to the saint by an otter). During the battle, Suibhne is driven mad by the noise, killing, and destruction, and flees to the woods, where he spends many years wandering naked, just as the saint had cursed. During this long period, he composes verses describing his deprivations and realizations. He describes himself as a bird. Several times he is found by his kinsmen and taken back to his kingdom, where he regains his senses; but each time something happens that sends him mad again, and he once more flees to the haven of the trees.

On one occasion, Suibhne crosses over to Scotland, where he meets another naked, tree-living madman called Ealadhan, and they share poems and experiences. Eventually, back in Ireland, Suibhne is taken in by St. Moling, who looks after him. A man named Mongan eventually spears Suibhne, whom he wrongly believes is having an affair with his wife. St. Moling blesses the madman and commends his body to Heaven, whereupon he dies.

Many of these incidents, and the general theme of the legend, are similar to descriptions about the lives of other well-known shamen, such as Merlin and the Scottish madman Lailoken. These were probably based on stories of early tribal shamen, who donned cloaks of bird feathers, went mad, and took to the trees during periods of Otherworld traveling. It will be beneficial to your study of tree magic to have a look at Suibhne's prophetic utterances, recorded in the form of nature poetry. I shall be using J. G. O'Keefe's translation as published by the Irish Texts Society (Volume 12), as this is the fullest and most comprehensive I have come across. The interpretations that follow are my own, and will serve to guide you to an understanding of this type of analysis. When you are ready, revisit this and other legends, and form your own interpretations of their meanings for your life and Work.

According to the legend, after Suibhne first went mad,

> for a long time thereafter he was faring throughout Ireland visiting and searching in high, rocky clefts and in bushy branches of tall ivy trees.

Suibhne's period of "visiting and searching" is specified as lasting one year. This is an initiatory period during which the shaman undergoes the hardships that give him the ability to communicate with the powers and energies of the Green World. The "high, rocky clefts" symbolize the struggle to reach upward for knowledge, and the "bushy branches of tall ivy trees" symbolize the knowledge of all of the trees, and how to use them in combination. Once his year of searching is over, we are told:

> He happened one night to be on the top of a tall ivy-clad hawthorn tree. It was hard for him to endure that bed, for every twist and turn he would give, a shower of thorns of the hawthorn would stick to him. Suibhne therefore changed from that bed to another place where there was a dense thicket of great briars with fine thorns and a single protruding branch of blackthorn growing alone up through the thicket.

The hawthorn symbolizes the inevitable backlash to be expected from successful magical Working. This is what is happening to poor Suibhne. He has successfully completed his year of studying the trees of the Tree Ogham, and now has to go through the period of balancing that this influx of knowledge and energy brings with it. He eases things a little by using his tree knowledge to invoke the help of the briar to clear away all the pieces that are no longer needed. He combines this sweeping action with the effects of the blackthorn, which represents the Otherworld and movement between the two worlds, to ease his transition from his Otherworld state of mind, where he has been for a year, to his normal state of mind.

The rest of the text describes the many places that Suibhne visited, and the people he encountered. When he felt threatened during these wanderings, or when he was being pursued, he always took refuge in a yew tree. The yew symbolizes the pinnacle of achievement, and the person who uses the yew, or in this case shelters in it, is one who has achieved all there is to know about the Tree Ogham. Suibhne was entitled to shelter in the yew, and avoid people who knew little or nothing of the powers and energies of the trees.

At one point in the story, he is tricked into returning to his kingdom and is held there in bonds. During this period his senses return to him, which means he temporarily gives up his shamanic ways and starts to resume a normal life. An old woman goads him into talking about his life in the forest, and asks to see a display of his amazing feats of agility (Suibhne is credited as having been as light as a bird, and able to leap from treetop to treetop without breaking branches). Suibhne gives in to the old hag, and leaps free from his bondage. Inevitably, his madness returns, and he must take to the trees in his shaman guise. It is at this point that he utters the longest poem in the story, sixty-five verses of four lines each. It contains many tree references, and part of it reads:

Thou oak, bushy, leafy,

thou art high beyond trees;

O hazlet, little branching one,

O fragrance of hazelnuts.

O alder, thou art not hostile,

delightful is thy hue,

thou art not rending and prickling

in the gap wherein thou art.

O little blackthorn, little thorny one;

O little black sloe-tree;

O watercress, little green topped one,

from the brink of the spring.

O apple tree, little apple tree,

much art thou shaken;

O quicken, little berried one,

delightful is thy bloom.

O briar, little arched one,

thou grantest no fair terms,

thou ceasest not to tear me,

till thou hast thy fill of blood.

O yew tree, little yew tree,

in churchyards thou art conspicuous;

O ivy, little ivy,

thou art familiar in the dusky wood.

O holly, little sheltering one,

thou door against the wind;

O ash tree, thou baleful one,

hand weapon of a warrior.

O birch, smooth and blessed,

thou melodious, proud one,

delightful each entwining branch

in the top of thy crown.

The aspen a-trembling;

by turns I hear

its leaves a-racing—

meseems 'tis the foray!

My aversion in woods—

I conceal it not from anyone—

is the leafy stirk of an oak

swaying evermore.

The rest of the poem enumerates the many places where Suibhne had found shelter, the many birds of the air he has seen, and the many animals of the forest he has encountered. It may well be that these places, birds, and animals are other forms of Ogham as discussed in Chapter One, which may also contain hidden information.

The first tree named in this poem is the oak, which is the sheltering defense and the protecting chief discussed in Chapter Eleven. It is what Suibhne needs after his long period of deprivation and captivity. The oak also represents the High King and the Sovereignty of the Land, which clearly applies to Suibhne on both levels. He was the political King of Dal Araidhe before his wanderings started; now he has achieved so much on a higher level that he has become his own spiritual High King, linked to the land. The oak is also closely associated with the Lord of the Hunt, and Suibhne appears to have become a Lord of the Hunt himself. The use of the oak sums up what has happened so far.

The next tree, the hazel, represents the death of the old self to clear the way for new knowledge and new experience. Suibhne's involvement and flight from the Battle of Magh Rath symbolizes this death. The deprivations which followed resulted in his gaining his new knowledge of the trees. He refers to the hazel a second time, as "little branching one." Several other trees are referred to twice in the poem, first by their name, and then with the adjective "little." The use of this word, in Irish poems and legends, is a term of endearment. Its use here shows us that Suibhne has an intimate relationship with these trees (the state for which we, too, strive).

The hazel leads to the next tree, the alder, which is the shield carried by the warrior, who has gained the protection of the spirit of the trees and can safely go forward and break new ground. The poem says of the alder, "thou art not hostile...thou art not rending and prickling." This is a reminder that the alder shield should be used only for defense. The line referring to the alder as being in "a gap" describes where Suibhne is. He has attained knowledge about the trees, but he must go even deeper into his shamanic studies. He is standing in a gap between the knowledge he has gained so far and the knowledge he has yet to encounter. The protective shield of alder fills the gap between him and the new experiences which lie ahead, which include the full knowledge and understanding of the blackthorn.

The blackthorn tree represents the need to face up to and prepare for your own death. By this stage, Suibhne will have realized that he cannot understand the trees fully on the physical level alone; it will be necessary for him to go to the higher levels to progress further. This symbolic death is a severe hardship for Suibhne, as his tale graphically relates. Because an action is purely symbolic does not make it any easier to do. In this case, facing up to his death causes Suibhne a considerable amount of pain. He does die in that his old way of life is gone forever.

When magical and symbolic acts are carried out correctly and sincerely, they have just as strong an effect as would the physical act. The introduction of watercress immediately after the naming of the blackthorn is a way of giving comfort to Suibhne, letting him know that everything will be all right. In early Irish literature, watercress was always associated with madmen and usually described as the only food they would eat. The significance of this may have something to do with the fact that the watercress has half of its existence under water, and half reaching to the light; the way a madman or shaman lives half in the watery realms of the Otherworld, and half striving for enlightenment in this world.

When Suibhne temporarily loses his senses, the apple tree is there to help and comfort him. The apple is a "shelter for a lunatic" and linked to death, the blackthorn, as the time when a madman's senses return to him. The apple's introduction at this point shows its use and significance on a practical, magical level. It is also the key to the Otherworld, and the symbol of those entitled to travel between the worlds. This is the state that Suibhne has achieved, clearly earning his apple branch.

Suibhne used the term, "little apple tree," indicating his closeness and fondness. The description, "much art thou shaken," is a reference to this as the tree most invoked by people attempting to gain the full powers of the shaman. Apple branches are also described in legends as being fitted with little bells and shaken in the presence of those about to undergo Otherworld journeys.

The rowan is named next, and symbolizes magical power, Otherworld visions, and the gaining of new knowledge. It also symbolizes the Lord of the Hunt and the acceptance of the two sides of the Green World. This is the severe test of accepting the ugly, harsh, and cruel aspects of the Green World, along with the beautiful, soft, and comforting aspects. Suibhne describes this stage in his deeply symbolic poem. Note the agony that he is experiencing. These experiences are very real, and are highlighted by the next tree, which in this translation is the briar. The Irish word used in the poem, *dhriseog*, means any plant with thorns capable of cutting flesh and causing pain. This could be the briar, bramble, or thorn bush. Here we have the dark side of the Green World, which Suibhne must recognize and accept. Suibhne tells us how hard this is: "grantest no fair terms…ceasest not to tear…and hast thy fill of blood." You, too, will have to face up to this tearing and scratching to progress through the Tree Ogham. There is no shortcut around the thorn bush; you must push through it, and come out the other side cut and bleeding, but wiser and braver.

Suibhne's success at coming to terms with this is shown by the next two trees, the yew and the ivy. The yew represents the pinnacle of success, and the ivy represents the power and knowledge of all of the trees. Having undergone all of the shaman's hardships, deprivations, and torments, Suibhne can now use the yew, as may only those who have reach this level. His knowledge of each tree, what it can do, and what it can be used for, is symbolized by the ivy; but the ivy also warns him not to become too self-assured—there is always more to learn. If you do not pay attention to this warning, the ivy will bind you until you are totally incapable of further progress. Suibhne is well aware of this, and introduces the ivy into his instructive poem at just the right place.

The ivy and the holly are evergreens, which symbolize the continuation of life. The holly represents the *Tainaiste,* or substitute for the High King, for those not yet capable of being their own High King. It also represents the need for self-sacrifice for further progress. Suibhne is capable of acting as his own High King, so the holly's aspect of substitution is not what is meant here. Its introduction is, instead, a warning to Suibhne that there are more self-sacrifices needed. This is confirmed by the further pains and hardships Suibhne soon endures. He refers to the holly as "little *sheltering* one," a description which is not given in any of the Word Oghams, but which is quite specific in this context. All of the trees described as shelters, such as the apple and the oak, are trees which also test the aspiring magician or shaman. In doing so, they also offer protection to those brave enough to face them. The holly is not normally a severe tester, but it is in this instance. Suibhne calls upon its balancing, gentler side to help him through the tests he is about to endure. This is also the meaning of his phrase, "thou door against the wind."

The trials and tests so vividly described in the poem are brought about by the next tree, the ash, which symbolizes progress through positive action. Suibhne has a choice here. He could quite legitimately decide he has had enough, and go no farther. He has achieved a great deal so far, and may decide that he is content with what he has. He may decide to progress to a new level of development. The next three trees provide indication as to what further progress may involve.

The first of these is the birch, which represents progress through self-sacrifice and pushing farther and higher than you have ever done before. It may be surprising to see the birch introduced here, as it is the first tree of the Tree Ogham, but any tree can be introduced at any time once all of the tree meanings have been learned and understood. In Suibhne's case, he knows more about the trees than any of us ever shall. Introducing the birch at this level shows that even he can go farther, if he is willing to put up with yet more hardships.

All this talk of hardships, deprivations, and self-sacrifice may cause you to ask, is it all worth it? Is there no other way to progress satisfactorily through the Tree Ogham? There are many ways through the forest of the Tree Ogham that are not as hard as the path Suibhne is experiencing. What we are studying is an ancient instruction intended for the ears of would-be tribal shamen, who would be expected to take on responsibility for the well-being and progress of the whole tribe's spiritual level. Such a person had to be totally capable and knowledgeable to be trusted with such responsibility. It is highly unlikely that any of us will ever be called upon to take on such an onerous task, but the principles remain the same: We must all expect a certain amount of trial and testing, and a certain degree of self-sacrifice, if we are to progress on our own spiritual paths. Suibhne gently reminds us of the fact that this is advantageous, no matter how unpleasant it is at the time. He describes this higher use of the birch as "smooth and blessed, thou melodious, proud one, delightful each entwining branch in the top of thy crown." There is always purpose and reason behind suffering and pain.

The next tree named, the aspen, represents the acknowledgment and acceptance of Suibhne's achievements. This is Suibhne's other choice—to sit back and accept what he has achieved, and be content with that. Sooner or later we will all face this same choice. You will find that it is not an easy decision to make. Some people will think, "Oh yes, I want to progress further, there is no doubt in my mind about that"; but others will be more cautious, look at what they have achieved, and think, "I have gained all that I need for the time being, and I am content with that." Neither of these is better than the other. Your aspirations and circumstances will dictate your choice when the time comes. There is never any need to make an instant decision when the consequences will last for a very long time. Should you decide to remain where you are, there is no reason why you cannot change your mind and, years later, resume your studies and return to the thicket of trees, its knowledge, and its tests.

The last tree in this sequence, the oak, is also the first tree to be named. This brings us back to where we started, but on a higher level, and shows us that in all things, including life itself, we shall eventually come back to where we started. We then must make our choice about whether to stay or to go on. As the rest of this legend relates, Suibhne decided to go deeper into his shamanic studies, and voluntarily underwent more deprivations and madness. The rest of the poem relates his hardships, but this time using places, animals, and birds instead of trees. This may be an instruction using Fortress Ogham, Animal Ogham, or Bird Ogham, as suggested in Chapter One.

From this examination of only one section of one poem, it is clear that the legend of Suibhne is a detailed description of the training of the shamen of the Celtic tribes. Part of this training involved a full understanding and working knowledge of the Tree Ogham. The need for shamen in today's society has all but disappeared, and there are very few people capable of undergoing the full training and initiation such a discipline demands. All of us, however, are capable of learning at least a little bit about the Tree Ogham and of using it in practical ways to help ourselves progress on all three levels, and to help others do the same. This makes the suffering and discomfort more than worthwhile.

Practical Work

My final suggestion concerning your Practical Work is to build an indoor Working area. This should be an area of your home, not necessarily an entire room, which will be a focus for your energies and those of the Green World. This area should be well lit, free from material objects other than a small table or other flat surface, with a plain, blank wall behind it. You will find as you progress that items will naturally gravitate to this area; but it should be free of the objects that were previously kept there.

After all the emphasis about going out into the Green World to learn to communicate with the trees in their own environment, you may wonder why I am now advocating an indoor Working area. My reasons are very practical ones. Some people, for various physical reasons, may find it impossible to Work outside their home. Some may have to travel considerable distances, perhaps at great expense, simply to get into a wild area of the Green World. These people will benefit from their own indoor Working area, their own indoor forest. Everyone, however, capable or incapable of travel, will find times when they need to communicate with a certain tree or trees and cannot make the journey to where the tree lives. This may be a result of some other magical Work, or of a strong and immediate intuitive feeling, or of a remembered dream of great significance.

The way to open this area is to spend a few days realizing that this otherwise ordinary part of your living space will soon be taking on a new and special importance. Prepare yourself mentally for a week or so before physically cleaning out the area. Once you have prepared it physically and mentally, bring in the spiritual level by starting to place your Ogham sticks in the area. Do this one stick per day, giving you almost a month to build up the energy of the place. Bring your sticks into your Working area in any order you like. It could be in the order given in the Tree Ogham, the order in which you came across them in your Green World journeys, or a haphazard, random order. Use your intuition, not your logical mind, for this task.

Your Ogham sticks will become physical links with the trees of the forest, which are thriving and Working in their own individual places outside. You will find that you can use them as talismen— magical objects which immediately link you with the greater forces and energies they represent. Hold them in your lap as you make

243

Otherworld journeys into the higher realms of the Tree Ogham. You may find you can develop ways to introduce them into more formal ritual Working, or you may find that you can simply cast your gaze upon them to the exclusion of all else, and simply open yourself to what comes through. You may also find that you can use them as a divinatory tool, whose meanings are displayed in the way they fall when tossed into the air, or in the order you pick them at random from beneath a piece of cloth. You can devise your own way of picking them at random, and develop a sense of connected meaning from the order in which they appear, in a manner similar to reading the Tarot cards. The Appendix provides a synopsis of each tree's meaning as an aid for you to use your Ogham sticks in this fashion.

Allow your Ogham sticks to sit on your table, where they will be in physical view. You will find that some naturally appear on the table, while others remain hidden away in their special place. Take note of these things, and see if you can determine any patterns as they come and go over the months and years. Are other objects attracted to this area as well? Things like personal belongings, photographs, pieces of jewelry, stones, shells, or other parts of the Green World may become relevant to the Work you are doing, and have a rightful place on your Work surface. You may find it helpful to place a drawing or photograph of the full tree on the blank wall behind your table to improve visualization. You can also hang drawings and representations of the characters and deities from legends as a visual aid to Otherworld communication.

Try to develop a sense of fluidity and freedom when using your indoor Working area. Let things happen naturally and open yourself up as much as you can to what you are told.

As you read the legends and become familiar with the characters and deities, you will note that many of them are connected with certain trees. Use these trees to the temporary exclusion of others when attempting conscious contact with these people. Lay the appropriate Ogham stick on your table and concentrate on it before starting Otherworld journeys in which you will make contact with your chosen character or deity. Many other uses and techniques will occur to you as you learn to Work both indoors and outdoors with the trees. Develop your own rituals and systems of Working, and become as close and familiar with each tree as possible.

Because these Ogham sticks will become Magical Weapons, you may want to devise a ritual or ceremony to dedicate and consecrate them to your Work. This will help charge them with extra energy, and will help you realize their importance. Your ritual need not be elaborate; it is the intention of the ritual which is most important. It may be helpful to place your Lesser Magical Weapons on the table at their appropriate quarters as you carry out your magical Work with the sticks.

The scope of this Practical Work is enormous. Despite its apparent simplicity, you will find useful, practical, and workable instruction, information, and guidance on all aspects of your life as you Work with the trees. These guidelines are merely suggestions based on a Practical Working system I have developed over the years, and which works for me. You may and should develop your own exercises and techniques to connect with the trees. The above suggestions will help you set your foot on the proper path. Have a long, safe, and pleasant journey.

CHAPTER TWENTY-SEVEN

TREES NOT LISTED IN THE TREE OGHAM

Although the Tree Ogham gives a very comprehensive account of the names, uses, meanings, and magical properties of twenty trees, this is only a fraction of the trees that exist in the Green World. What of the other common European and American species such as the beech, the chestnut, the sycamore, and the elm? What of the other bushes and creepers, which seem to be of equal importance to the Green World? Why are they not included in this magical system?

The answer to these questions is twofold: One, the number of trees must coincide with the number of notches used in the Ogham script. To fit more trees into the system would require the introduction of more notches, and this would produce a cumbersome and impractical system. This was attempted with the introduction of the *forfeda*, but, as we have seen, these letters are superfluous to a workable and manageable system.

The other reason is that many of the trees and shrubs that now adorn our countryside and gardens are not native to the Celtic lands and were, therefore, unknown to the creators of this system. Many of the plants we now accept as integral parts of our landscape were introduced by immigrants, who brought them from their native lands. They also introduced birds and other animals that, until their arrival, had not been known in the British Isles.

This is humankind playing the same role as the birds and animals in spreading seeds and establishing new growth. A bird will eat fruit from a tree, fly many hundreds of miles, and deposit the seed in its droppings. Land-dwelling animals, too, will eat plants and trees, carry their seeds in their stomachs for days, and release them far from their host plant. Humankind, with its ability to cross the globe with ease, is probably the biggest carrier of seeds and plants the Green World has ever known. This cross-fertilization also applies to our own species. We carry our human seed and mix it with members of other races to produce a wonderful amalgam of colors and creeds. This is the natural progression experienced by all living things in the Green World.

The trees with which we are now familiar are not the trees our Celtic forebears knew. How do we, then, Work tree magic to the full, yet not attempt to resurrect a system that is no longer relevant? The answer to this is again twofold: First, the Tree Ogham is still relevant for the simple reason that the trees identified within this system are still to be found; and second, the Tree Ogham should be seen as a basis upon which to learn how to Work with trees and other growing and living things of the Green World. There is no reason why you should not use the techniques described here to examine non-Ogham trees, and to learn of their unique properties and uses. This will take a great deal of effort and experimentation, but it is something you must do if you are to progress and pass on information to those who come after you.

The simplest way to break this new ground might be to take a detailed look at the *forfeda*. Quite a lot of information can be obtained from other books on Ogham. I have listed some of these in the Bibliography. The real test is to go out into the Green World, find a beech or elm, sit down next to it and, using the skills and knowledge of the Green World and the other trees, feel what this new tree is like. Open up to it on the Otherworld level and start to communicate with it and the area in which it is growing. See if you can identify its unique purpose. If you think back to the trees of the Tree Ogham, you will remember that each tree serves a very specific purpose. It is now up to you to find out what the purposes of the non-Ogham trees are. Do not limit yourself. The life forms of the Green World are varied beyond comprehension. The information we can extract from them is limitless. Some books dealing with Tree Ogham will tell you that non-Alphabet trees should be ignored, but this is ridiculous. When you examine the Tree Ogham in detail, it becomes clear that its composers never intended it to remain static, but to grow, develop, and expand just like every other facet of the Green World it represents.

Spend time studying the trees, shrubs, and plants of your neck of the woods that are not named in the Tree Ogham. Remember that the Tree Ogham is only one of over a hundred different basic Oghams; there is no reason why you could not develop your own system, based on something which has never before been set to the Ogham notches. I would strongly suggest, however, that before you leap into the exciting world of free-form experimentation, you get a firm grip on the branches and trunks of the trees of the Tree Ogham on all three levels. Before any tree can grow, it must have its roots securely embedded in the earth. This is lesson for you, my friends. Get a good grip on the powers and energies of this world before you start branching out to new and uncharted lands. You may find that the twenty trees of the Tree Ogham give you more than enough to cope with for this lifetime. If this is the case, then so be it. Listen to your intuition and follow its wise and sound guidance.

DIVINATION USING OGHAM STICKS

Divination with Ogham sticks works best with questions of magical Working. I have not found them to be very helpful in answering questions relating to the mundane world. Divination may be the wrong term to use here. The Ogham sticks do not define the future, but help you to see situations in their fullest possible context. This is often all that is needed for you to decide on your own future actions.

There is no right or wrong way to using Ogham sticks as a divinatory tool. The only guideline I would give is that any system you devise must be based on a random selection of the sticks. This could be done by throwing them into the air and seeing how they fall. You could then decide on their importance according to which one is on top, which one is next, and so on. This would also give you a random placement of trees relative to each other. Another way to choose sticks would be to place them inside a bag and pull them out, one by one, in a random fashion. This would also give you an order of importance and the relative position of the trees.

If you are using the sticks to answer questions posed by a third party, you might ask that person to give you a list of numbers between one and twenty, and pick each tree according to its order in the Tree Ogham alphabet. You could also ask the third party to recite as many trees names as he or she can and, from this list, pick the ones that are part of the Tree Ogham, in the order named.

As you become more familiar with the Ogham sticks while Working with them in this manner, they will start to provide more meaning that will be sparked by the sight of the Ogham stick and its attendant symbolism, but which will actually be coming from your Higher Self and your Otherworld guide. This is how a good Tarot reader operates, allowing the image of each card to trigger the appropriate symbolism, but allowing a certain amount of intuition to come into play as well.

What follows are simple groups of meanings for each tree as a quick reference to their main attributes. Remember that these attributes will change depending upon the relative position of the other trees(s). This is where the notes in your magical diary will prove useful.

BIRCH: New beginnings; change to a higher level; self-sacrifice for the common good; devotion to the Great Work.

ROWAN: Magical work; concentrated Inner effort needed.

ALDER: Going forth to conquer adversaries or difficulties; finding the strength to face up to things you have been avoiding.

WILLOW: New journeys; Otherworld contacts; confidence in what you are doing, even though it seems wrong or doubtful.

ASH: Inertia; boredom or lethargy needing to be broken; change of outlook needed; difficult time; extra effort needed.

HAWTHORN: Unpleasant period about to happen; ultimately signifies success; a completion of something.

OAK: Higher powers at work; time to rest from action; your own spiritual aspect.

HOLLY: Substitution; things are not what they seem; a middle period between two opposites; a new guide about to appear.

HAZEL: Death; change; wisdom.

APPLE: Awakening of Otherworld senses; work in hand is protected; spiritual Work coming to fruition.

VINE: Hidden knowledge; overcoming adversaries by Otherworld strength; inspiration.

IVY: Warnings; think twice about what you are doing; restrictions.

BROOM: Incompletion; further Work needed to complete the project; time to clear away what is no longer needed or is outdated; learn from past mistakes.

BLACKTHORN: Be prepared for a transition; prepare for something about to end; sudden change; death.

ELDER: Face up to the truth; time for self-examination and honesty.

FIR: Look at how you fit into relationships; a broad range of experience; new realizations about to make themselves known.

FURZE: Time to kill; resistance is going to be felt; try to see what is being born from the immediate difficulty.

HEATHER: Responsibility; time to examine what you are doing—are you sure you are ready for the consequences?; new life; a baby.

ASPEN: Spiritual achievement; great success; be wary of becoming too big-headed; protection.

YEW: Love (this Ogham stick can also indicate you should reconsider the other sticks on a higher level or, if it feels right, draw them all again).

AONGHUS (ah-nish). Irish Celtic god of love, also a trickster character.

BEALTAINE (bal-tayn). One of the four major festivals of the Irish Celts. This festival heralded the start of summer and was celebrated at the beginning of the growing season, now standardized to the first of May.

BEITHE LUIS NION. The Old Irish name for the Tree Alphabet, similar to "A–B–C" being used today to refer to the English Alphabet.

BOBEL LOTH ALPHABET. An alphabet which, as far as we know, was unused, and was based on the names of mythical teachers and scholars.

BRIGHID (bree-yid). Irish Celtic goddess associated with smithcraft, healing, and poetry. Still a very popular figure in Ireland and West Scotland today.

CATH (kah). A battle. One of the main classes of tales. Some twenty battle-tales are known, the most famous being Cath Maige Tured (kah moytura), the Battle of Moytura (for a full examination of the magical content of this legend, see my book *The Irish Celtic Magical Tradition*); Cath Maige Mucrime (kah moy mucrame), the Battle of Moy Mucrame.

CELTS/CELTIC. Originally the Celtic countries and peoples covered a vast area of Europe and parts of Asia, but for the purposes of this book, I am only concerned with the peoples and practices found in ancient and modern Ireland, and the West of Scotland.

COPPICED. The practice of cutting back trees to encourage new growth.

CORACLE. A small wooden-framed boat, usually covered in leather, used by the Celts of Scotland, Ireland, and Wales.

DRUID. Member of the most important caste in Celtic Ireland. Not the keepers of the Celtic religion, as is usually assumed, but more lawmakers, advice-givers, and magical practitioners. There were also Druidesses in Ireland.

DRUIDIC ORDER. The Druidic caste or sect which existed in all Celtic societies.

FEDA (fay-dah). The Old Irish word meaning "letters," specifically of the Ogham alphabet.

FIANNA. An Old Irish word which means "warriors." Now used to refer to the mythical band of roving Celtic warriors who acted much as a modern police force. They were under the leadership of Fionn mac Cumhaill, The Fianna patrolled both Ireland and Western Scotland.

FINDIAS. One of the four Otherworld cities where the Tuatha De Danann were taught their magical skills before arriving in Ireland. Nuadhu's sword was brought from this city.

FIONN. An Old Irish word which means "white" and has its roots in the ancient word for "knowledge." Fionn mac Cumhaill was the leader of the Fianna and the body of tales known as The Fenian Cycle all deal with Fionn and the Fianna.

FLESC (flayshk). The Old Irish word used to describe the actual notches on stone, wood, etc., used when writing the Ogham alphabet.

FOMHOIRE (foh-voy-rah). A mysterious race of non-humans who allegedly settled in Ireland before being driven out by the Tuatha De Danann. They are usually described as being evil and dangerous.

FORFEDA (fore-fay-dah). The "supplementary" characters of the Ogham alphabet which seem too have been added to the original 20 at a later date.

GEIS (gaysh), plural geasa (gaysha). A prohibition or taboo placed upon someone, usually the High King, which defined what he or she could or could not do. A very important part of many legends and also in the real life of the ordinary Celt. Some geasa were connected with totem animals, some with certain aspects of hospitality, some with journeys and traveling but, whatever the geis concerned, should a person wittingly or unwittingly break it, then certain doom would follow.

GORIAS. One of the four Otherworld cities where the Tuatha De Danann received their magical training before coming to Ireland. "From Gorias was brought the spear which Lugh had."

GREAT YEAR. A period of roughly 19 years during which the Moon will complete its full cycle of the Earth before returning to the same rising place on the horizon.

GREEN WORLD. Equivalent to the more common term World of Nature, but including the mineral kingdom as well as the plant and animal kingdoms of this world. A very important, but often neglected, aspect of the Irish Celtic magical tradition.

GRIMOIRES. The medieval name for magical text books. It comes from a corruption of the English word "Grammars."

GUIDE. A general term used to describe anyone or anything from the Otherworld who appears during an Otherworld journey and offers assistance. Some guides may appear regularly, and you may strike up a real bond of friendship with them, while others may only appear for one particular Working and never be encountered again. They should always be treated with respect and courtesy, and thanked for their assistance.

KEENING. The practice of wailing and crying noisily to lament the death of someone. Said to have been invented by Brighid.

KENNINGS. A word or phrase used by druids, bards, and poets to describe in highly symbolic language people, places, or things. (e.g. "the Plain of Tethra" is a kenning for the ocean. "The Cattle of the Plain of Tethra" is a kenning for fish and "The Man who tends the Cattle of the Plain of Tethra" is a kenning for a fisherman.)

LAY (lay). A poem or song.

LIA FAIL (lee-ah-foyl). The Stone of Destiny which had been brought from the Otherworld city of Falias, and which stood at Tara. Its function was to declare the true High King of Ireland by screaming aloud when the successful candidate stood upon it. The stone which stands at Tara today is probably not the original.

MAGICAL DIARY. A personal notebook kept to record details of Otherworld journeys or rituals carried out during your Practical Work. It is by keeping such a diary accurately and meticulously that you will be able to gauge your progress and learn in the years to come. The diary can also be used to record any coincidences which occur in your day-to-day life, or any thoughts, realizations, or ideas that may come to you at any time of day or night, which may be of importance later.

MAGICAL WEAPONS. There are two sets of Magical Weapons: the Greater Weapons, which are the Spear, Sword, Cauldron, and Shield; and the Lesser Weapons, which are the Wand, Knife, Cup, and Stone. These are the basic implements with which all ritual Work is carried out. The Greater Weapons are used in large, group Workings, usually outside, whereas the Lesser Weapons are used for small, personal Workings either inside or outside.

MARQUETRY. The process of inlaying wood with other strips of wood to create decorative designs.

MORAINN. Chief judge and important druid of the Ulster Cycle.

MURIAS. One of the four Otherworld cities where the Tuatha De Danann were taught their magical skills before they came to Ireland. The Daghdha's ever-full cauldron was brought from here.

OGHAM (oh-am). Ancient form of writing consisting of various notches across the straight edge of a stick or standing stone. Although by tradition it is closely associated with magic, the only known authentic Ogham inscriptions are all dedications to dead warriors and the like. Said to have been invented by the god Oghma, the god of eloquence. The original Ogham may actually have been a very formalized way of asking and answering questions. Associated with the Tree Alphabet.

OGHAM STICKS. Short pieces of different woods carved or painted with their appropriate Ogham letter used in a form of divination.

OGHMA (oh-ma). Irish Celtic god of strength and eloquence.

OGMIOS (oy-mos). Gaulish Celtic god of strength and eloquence.

OTHERWORLD. The non-physical realms which interlock with this world, but which are not obvious to the physical senses. The world of the deities and non-human beings who inhabit our universe. More often referred to as the Inner Levels nowadays.

PICT. An ancient Celtic people who once occupied the North East of Scotland, and probably parts of Ireland, who have since vanished without any trace other than a few historical references to them and their tantalizing Ogham stones.

PICTISH. Of the Picts

POLLARDED. A method of cutting back trees to encourage growth similar to coppicing but not quite so severe.

RUNES (roons). An ancient alphabet used by Germanic, Teutonic, and Scandinavian peoples.

SAMHAIN (sow-in). One of the four major festivals of the Celts, which signified the end of summer and the start of the new year. A very magical time. Nowadays standardized to October 31 and November 1, and celebrated as Hallowe'en. A feast of the dead, and a time for much magic to be Worked for the forthcoming year.

SATIRE. A short poem pointing out a person's faults or bad characteristics designed to shame that person into changing.

SHILLELAGH. A traditional wooden club in Ireland made from the part of the tree where the branch leaves the main trunk.

SID. Singular form of SIDHE.

SIDHE (shee). An all-encompassing term, which originally referred to the underground dwellings of the fairy people, but is used here to designate the fairies or non-human Otherworld inhabitants themselves.

TAEBOMNAI (tay-bow-nih). The consonants of the Ogham alphabet.

TAIN (toyn). A plundering expedition, usually in the form of a cattle raid. One of the main classes of tales. We know the names of at least fourteen of these raids. The most famous is the great Tain Bo Cuailnge (toyn boh Cooley), the Cattle Raid of Cooley.

TARA. The seat of the High King where the Lia Fail stood. Also given as Teamhair (tah-var). The spiritual center of Ireland.

TAROT CARDS. An ancient deck of cards consisting of a group of 22 picture cards plus four suits of 14 cards each similar to a modern deck of playing cards. Used today mainly for divination purposes.

TREE CALENDAR. A calendar aligned to the Tree Alphabet by associating each month of the year with a tree. A relatively modern invention.

TREE OGHAM. One of the many alphabets of Ogham, this one being specifically associated with trees.

TUATHA DE DANANN (too-ah dje dahnahn). The People of the Goddess Danu—a race of gods and goddesses who made up virtually the whole of the Irish and Scottish Celtic pantheon.

ULSTER CYCLE. A body of stories centered on King Conchobhar mac Neasa and his Knights of the Red Branch who were based at Eamhain Mhacha in Ulster—hence the name of this cycle of mythology.

WATTLE. A framework of interwoven sticks and twigs used to make walls and partitions.

WORD OGHAM. A series of kennings used to describe each letter of the Ogham alphabet.

BIBLIOGRAPHY

Bellingham, D. *An Introduction to Celtic Mythology*. London: The Apple Press, 1990.

Berresford Ellis, P. *A Dictionary of Irish Mythology*. London: Constable, 1987.

Blamires, S. *The Irish Celtic Magical Tradition*. London: The Aquarian Press, 1992.

———. *Glamoury: Magic of the Celtic Green World*. St Paul: Llewellyn, 1995.

Book of Leinster Tain. Dublin: Irish Texts Society, 1969.

Buile Suibhne Geilt. Dublin: Irish Texts Society, 1913.

Caldecott, M. *Women in Celtic Myth*. London: Arrow Books, 1988.

Campbell, J. F. *Popular Tales of the West Highlands*. 4 Vols. Aldershot: Wildwood House, 1983.

Carmichael, A. *Carmina Gadelica*. Edinburgh: Floris Books, 1992.

Carr-Gomm, P. *The Elements of the Druid Tradition*. Shaftesbury: Element Books, 1991.

———. *The Druid Way*. Shaftesbury: Element Books, 1993.

———. *The Druid Animal Oracle Deck*. New York: Simon & Schuster, 1995.

Cath Maige Mucraime. Dublin: Irish Texts Society, 1975.

Cath Maige Tuired. Dublin: Irish Texts Society, 1983.

Chadwick, N. *The Celts*. London: Pelican, 1971.

Cross, T. P. & C. H. Slover. *Ancient Irish Tales*. Dublin: Figgis, 1936.

Cunliffe, B. *The Celtic World*. London: The Bodley Head, 1979.

Delaney, F. *The Celts*. London: BBC Publications, 1986.

———. *Legends of the Celts*. London: Hodder & Stoughton, 1989.

Dillon, M. *Cycles of the Irish Kings*. Oxford: Oxford University Press, 1946.

———. *Irish Sagas*. Dublin: Mercier, 1985.

Dillon, M. & N. Chadwick. *The Celtic Realms*. London: Wiedenfield & Nicolson, 1967.

Duanaire Finn. 3 Vols. Dublin: Irish Texts Society, 1908, 1933, 1954.

Fled Bricrend. Dublin: Irish Texts Society, 1899.

Forman, W. & V. Kruta. *The Celts of the West*. London: Orbis, 1985.

Gantz, J. *Early Irish Myths & Sagas*. London: Penguin, 1981.

Gregory, Lady Augusta. *Cuchulainn of Muirthemne*. Gerrards Cross: Smythe, 1984.

———. *Gods & Fighting Men*. Gerrards Cross: Smythe, 1979.

Harbison, P. *Pre-Christian Ireland*. London: Thames & Hudson, 1988.

Hull, E. *The Cuchulainn Saga*. London: George G. Harrap, 1911.

Jackson, K. *A Celtic Miscellany*. London: RKP, 1951.

Joyce, P. W. *Old Celtic Romances*. London: Kegan Paul, 1879.

———. *A Social History of Ancient Ireland*. Harlow: Longmans, 1903.

Keating, G. *The History of Ireland*. 4 Vols. Dublin: Irish Texts Society, 1902, 1908, 1914.

Kendrick, T. D. *The Druids*. Largs: Banton Press (reprints), 1990.

Kinsella, T. *The Tain*. Oxford: Oxford University Press, 1986.

Kruta, V. & et al., eds. *The Celts*. New York: Rizzoli, 1991.

Lebor Gabala Erenn. 5 Vols. Dublin: Irish Texts Society, 1938–56.

Lebor Na Cert. Dublin: Irish Texts Society, 1962.

MacCana, P. *Celtic Mythology*. London: Hamlyn, 1975.

———. *The Learned Tales of Medieval Ireland*. Dublin: Dublin Institute for Advanced Studies, 1980.

Macleod, F. *The Collected Works*. 7 Vols. London: Heinnemann, 1910.

Matthews, C. *The Elements of the Celtic Tradition*. Shaftesbury: Element Books, 1989.

———. *The Celtic Book of the Dead*. London: St. Martins Press, 1993.

Matthews, C. & J. *The Western Way*. 2 Vols. London: Arkana, 1985.

Matthews, J. *The Grail: Quest for Eternal Life*. London: Thames & Hudson, 1988.

———. *The Elements of the Arthurian Tradition*. Shaftesbury: Element Books, 1989.

———. *The Celtic Shaman*. Shaftesbury: Element Books, 1991.

———. *A Celtic Reader*. London: The Aquarian Press, 1990.

———. *Fionn MacCumhaill*. Dorset: Firebird Books, 1988.

Matthews, J. & C. *The Aquarian Guide to British and Irish Mythology.* London: The Aquarian Press, 1988.

Meyer, Kuno. *Death Tales of the Ulster Heroes.* Dublin: Hodges, 1906.

———. *The Voyage of Bran Son of Febal.* Dublin: Nutt, 1895.

Neeson, E. *1st Book of Irish Myths & Legends.* Dublin: Mercier, 1981.

———. *2nd Book of Irish Myths & Legends.* Dublin: Mercier, 1982.

Nichols, R. *The Book of Druidry.* London: The Aquarian Press, 1990.

O'Grady, S. H. *Silva Gadelica.* 2 Vols. Dublin: Williams & Norgate, 1892.

O'hOgain, D. *Myth, Legend & Romance.* New York: Ryan, 1991.

O'Rahilly, T. F. *Early Irish History & Mythology.* Dublin: Dublin Institute for Advanced Studies, 1946.

Powell, T. *The Celts.* London: Thames & Hudson, 1983.

Rees, A. & B. *Celtic Heritage.* London: Thames & Hudson, 1974.

Rhys, J. *The Hibbert Lectures.* Dublin: Williams & Norgate, 1888.

Rolleston, T. W. *Celtic Myths & Legends.* London: Bracken Books, 1985.

Ross, A. *Pagan Celtic Britain.* London: RKP, 1967.

———. *The Life & Death of a Druid Prince.* London: Rider, 1989.

Rutherford, W. *The Druids.* London: The Aquarian Press, 1983.

Sharkey, J. *Celtic Mysteries.* London: Thames & Hudson, 1975.

Smyth, D. *A Guide to Irish Mythology.* Dublin: Irish Academic Press, 1988.

Spence, L. *History & Origins of Druidism.* London: The Aquarian Press, 1971.

———. *Magic Arts in Celtic Britain.* London: The Aquarian Press, 1970.

Squire, C. *Celtic Myth & Legend.* Henley-on-Thames: Gresham, 1905.

Stewart, R. J. *Celtic Gods Celtic Goddesses.* London: Blandford, 1990.

———. *Cuchulainn.* Dorset: Firebird Books, 1988.

————. *The Underworld Initiation*. London: The Aquarian Press, 1988.

————. *Living Magical Arts*. London: Blandford Press, 1987.

————. *Advanced Magical Arts*. Shaftesbury: Element Books, 1988.

Toraidheacht Dhiarmada Agus Ghrainne. Dublin: Irish Texts Society, 1967.

Williamson, R. *The Craneskin Bag*. Edinburgh: Canongate, 1989.

Young, E. *Celtic Wonder Tales*. Edinburgh: Floris Books, 1983.

Ogham & The Tree Alphabet

Brash, R. B. *The Ogam Inscribed Monuments of the Gaedhil*. Dublin, 1879.

Calder, G. *Auraicept na nEces*. Edinburgh: Long, 1917.

Diack, F. C. *The Origin of the Ogam Alphabet*. Edinburgh: Scottish Gaelic Studies, Vol. 3, 1931.

Diringer, D. *The Alphabet, the Key to the History of Mankind*. London, 1968.

Elliott, R.W.V. *Runes, an Introduction*. London: RKP, 1980.

Fell, B. *America B.C.* New York: Pocket Books, 1989.

Jackson, K. H. *Language & History in Early Britain*. London: RKP, 1953.

Macalister, R.A.S. *The Secret Languages of Ireland*. Dublin: Mercier, 1937.

McManus, D. A *Guide to Ogam*. Maynooth: Maynooth Studies Series, 1991.

Wainwright F. T., ed. *The Problem of the Picts*. London: Penguin, 1980.

DISCOGRAPHY

Many traditional and contemporary Irish and Scottish singers and groups do not have worldwide record distribution and, consequently, readers outside of these countries may have difficulty obtaining some recordings. Most large record stores have an Import section where these might be found.

BLACK FAMILY (Frances, Martin, Mary, Michael and Shay). Irish family of two sisters and three brothers who have recorded many albums as a family, solo, and in various combinations.

CAPERCAILLIE. Scottish group who have released several excellent albums in both Gaelic and English.

CLANNAD. Irish group of sisters and brothers who have recorded many albums in Irish and English.

THE IRON HORSE. Contemporary Scottish group with a unique and very exciting sound, both on stage and in the studio.

DOUGIE MACLEAN. Scottish singer and songwriter who has written some fine contemporary pieces he performs with a delightful voice and mastery of the guitar and fiddle.

CHRISTY MOORE. Irish singer and songwriter of long standing, with a deep passion for his country and people. My favorite.

THE OLD BLIND DOGS. Contemporary Scottish group who are gaining a strong following on both sides of the Atlantic. Great live band.

PLANXTY. Irish band who are sadly now disbanded. During their heyday were probably one of the most influential bands to come out of Ireland.

RUNRIG. Outstanding contemporary Scottish rock group, who perform in both Gaelic and English, live and in the studio.

ALAN STIVELL. Breton harper and singer with a large, international following.

SULIS MUSIC AND TAPES. BCM Box 3721, London WC1N 3XX. Produce many musical and magical tapes of a very high standard.

THE TANNAHILL WEAVERS. One of the stalwarts of the traditional Scottish music scene, known internationally.

THE WHISTLEBINKIES. One of the very few groups to play genuinely traditional Scottish music on traditional Scottish instruments, as well as composing their own, contemporary pieces.

ROBIN WILLIAMSON. Produces excellent story tapes as well as excellent music. Write to Robin Williamson Productions, BCM 4797, London, WC1N 3XX, England, or P.O. Box 27522, Los Angeles, CA 90027, U.S.A. for full catalog.

JOURNALS AND SOCIETIES

Cambrian Medieval Celtic Studies, Department of Welsh, University of Wales, Aberystwyth, SY23 2AX, Wales.

Celtica (Journal of the School of Celtic Studies), 10 Burlington Road, Dublin 4, Ireland.

Dublin Institute for Advanced Studies, 10 Burlington Road, Dublin 4, Ireland.

Eigse, a Journal of Irish Studies, National University of Ireland, 49 Merrion Square, Dublin 2, Ireland.

Emania (Journal of the Navan Fort Research Group), Department of Archaeology, Queen's University, Belfast, BT7 1NN, N. Ireland.

Irish Texts Society, ‰ The Royal Bank of Scotland, Drummonds Branch, 49 Charing Cross, Admiralty Arch, London SW1A 2DX, England.

Order of Bards, Ovates, and Druids, PO Box 1333, Lewes, E. Sussex, BN7 3ZG, England.

Pagan Life, Newsletter of the Irish Pagan Movement, The Bridge House, Clonegal, Enniscorthy, Co. Wexford, Ireland.

Pas Newsletter, Pictish Arts Society, School of Scottish Studies, 27 George Square, Edinburgh, EH8 9LD, Scotland.

Shadow (Journal of the Traditional Cosmology Society), School of Scottish Studies, 27 George Square, Edinburgh, EH8 9LD, Scotland.

INDEX

☾ REACH FOR THE MOON

Llewellyn publishes hundreds of books on your favorite subjects! To get these exciting books, including the ones on the following pages, check your local bookstore or order them directly from Llewellyn.

Order by Phone
- Call toll-free within the U.S. and Canada, 1-877-NEW-WRLD
- In Minnesota, call (651) 291-1970
- We accept VISA, MasterCard, and American Express

Order by Mail
- Send the full price of your order (MN residents add 7% sales tax) in U.S. funds, plus postage & handling to:
  Llewellyn Worldwide
  P.O. Box 64383, Dept. 1-56718-070-1
  St. Paul, MN 55164–0383, U.S.A.

Postage & Handling
- **Standard** (U.S., Mexico, & Canada)

If your order is:

$20.00 or under, add $5.00

$20.01–$100.00, add $6.00

Over $100, shipping is free

(Continental U.S. orders ship UPS. AK, HI, PR, & P.O. Boxes ship USPS 1st class. Mex. & Can. ship PMB.)
- **Second Day Air** (Continental U.S. only): $10.00 for one book + $1.00 per each additional book
- **Express** (AK, HI, & PR only) [Not available for P.O. Box delivery. For street address delivery only.]: $15.00 for one book + $1.00 per each additional book
- **International Surface Mail:** Add $1.00 per item
- **International Airmail:** Books—Add the retail price of each item; Non-book items—Add $5.00 per item

Please allow 4–6 weeks for delivery on all orders.
Postage and handling rates subject to change.

Discounts
We offer a 20% discount to group leaders or agents. You must order a minimum of 5 copies of the same book to get our special quantity price.

Free Catalog
Get a free copy of our color catalog, *New Worlds of Mind and Spirit*. Subscribe for just $10.00 in the United States and Canada ($30.00 overseas, airmail). Call 1-877-NEW-WRLD today!

Visit our website at www.llewellyn.com for more information.

GLAMOURY
MAGIC OF THE CELTIC GREEN WORLD
Steve Blamires

Glamoury refers to an Irish Celtic magical tradition that is truly holistic, satisfying the needs of the practitioner on the physical, mental, and spiritual levels. This guidebook offers practical exercises and modern versions of time-honored philosophies that will expand your potential into areas previously closed to you.

We have moved so far away from our ancestors' closeness to the Earth—the Green World—that we have nearly forgotten some very important truths about human nature that are still valid. *Glamoury* brings these truths to light so you can take your rightful place in the Green World. View and experience the world in a more balanced, meaningful way. Meet helpers and guides from the Otherworld who will become your valued friends. Live in tune with the seasons and gauge your inner growth in relation to the Green World around you.

The ancient Celts couched their wisdom in stories and legends. Today, intuitive people can learn much from these tales. *Glamoury* presents a system based on Irish Celtic mythology to guide you back to the harmony with life's cycles that our ancestors knew.

1-56718-069-8, 6 x 9, 352 pp., illus., softcover   **$16.95**

OMENS, OGHAMS & ORACLES
DIVINATION IN THE DRUIDIC TRADITION
Richard Webster

Although hundreds of books have been written about the Celts and the druids, no book has focused exclusively on Celtic divination—until now. *Omens, Oghams & Oracles* covers the most important and practical methods of divination in the Celtic and druidic traditions, two of which have never before been published: an original system of divining using the druidic Ogham characters, and "Arthurian divination," which employs a geomantic oracle called druid sticks.

Even if you have no knowledge or experience with any form of divination, this book will show you how to create and use the 25 Ogham fews and the druid sticks to gain accurate and helpful insights into your life. This book covers divination through sky stones, touchstones, bodhran drums, and other means, with details on how to make these objects and sample readings to supplement the text. Beautiful illustrations of cards made from the Oghams, geomantic figures, and more, enhance this clear and informative book, which also includes chapters on the history, lives, and philosophy of the Celts and druids.

Many Celtic divinatory methods are as useful today as they were 2,000 years ago—make modern forms of these ancient oracles work for you!

1–56718–800–1, 7 x 10, 224 pp., softbound **$12.95**

CELTIC FOLKLORE COOKING
Joanne Asala

Celtic cooking is simple and tasty, reflecting the quality of its ingredients: fresh meat and seafood, rich milk and cream, fruit, vegetables, and wholesome bread. Much of the folklore, proverbs, songs, and legends of the Celtic nations revolve around this wonderful variety of food and drink. Now you can feast upon these delectable stories as you sample more than 200 tempting dishes with *Celtic Folklore Cooking*.

In her travels to Ireland, Wales, and Scotland, Joanne Asala found that many people still cook in the traditional manner, passing recipes from generation to generation. Now you can serve the same dishes discovered in hotels, bed and breakfasts, restaurants, and family kitchens. At the same time, you can relish in the colorful proverbs, songs, and stories that are still heard at pubs and local festivals and that complement each recipe.

1-56718-044-2, 264 pp., 7 x 10, illus.   **$17.95**

SCOTTISH WITCHCRAFT
THE HISTORY & MAGICK OF THE PICTS
Raymond Buckland

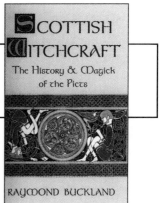

From the ancient misty Highlands of Scotland to modern-day America come the secrets of solitary Witchcraft practice. *Scottish Witchcraft* explores "PectiWita," or the craft of the Picts, the mysterious early Keltic people. The Scottish PectiWita tradition differs in many ways from the Wicca of England—there is little emphasis on the worship of the gods (though it is there), but more on the living and blending of magick into everyday life.

Many people attracted to modern-day Wicca are unable to contact or join a coven. PectiWita is a path for the solitary Witch; and here, for the first time, are full details of this solitary branch of the Old Ways. Learn the history of the Picts, their origins and beliefs. Learn how to make simple tools and use them to work magic. Through step-by-step instructions you are brought into touch and then into complete harmony with all of nature. Explore their celebrations, talismans, song and dance, herbal lore, runes and glyphs, and recipes. Learn how to practice the religion in the city and with groups. Ray Buckland's contact with the late Aidan Breac, a descendent of the Picts, led to his interest in Scottish Witchcraft and to writing this present volume.

0-87542-057-5, 256 pp., 5¼ x 8, illus., photos, softcover $9.95

DRUID MAGIC
THE PRACTICE OF CELTIC WISDOM
Maya Magee Sutton, Ph.D., &
Nicholas R. Mann
preface by Philip Carr-Gomm, Chief
Druid of OBOD

Enter into the adventure of awakening the Druid within. If you want to explore the Druid mysteries, this book will help you roll up your mystical sleeves. For those who want to know who the Celts and the Druids really were, this book presents the Celtic myths, Greek and Roman writings, and archaeological evidence that allows the ancient Druid tradition to speak for itself. If you want to learn the primary tenets of Druidry, or visit the Celtic Otherworlds and lie in the "streambed of Druidic inspiration," this book will take you on that journey.

- Create Druid magical tools
- Develop yourself as a seer
- Become a Druid magus
- Live your sacred sexuality
- Hold Druid ceremonies in your back yard
- Initiate yourself as a Peregrine Druid
- Form a Druid grove
- Visit the Celtic homelands
- Learn the Druid path from nature
- Use the Celtic Tree alphabet
- Journey to the Otherworlds
- Achieve Druid inspiration through poetry, symbols, visions, and spoken word

1-56718-481-2, 384 pp., 7½ x 9⅛ $14.95

IN THE SHADOW OF THE SHAMAN
CONNECTING WITH SELF, NATURE & SPIRIT
Amber Wolfe

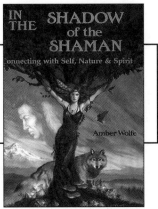

Presented in what the author calls a "cookbook shamanism" style, this book shares recipes, ingredients, and methods of preparation for experiencing some very ancient wisdoms: wisdoms of Native American and Wiccan traditions, as well as contributions from other philosophies of Nature as they are used in the shamanic way. Wheels, the circle, totems, shields, directions, divinations, spells, care of sacred tools, and meditations are all discussed. Wolfe encourages us to feel confident and free to use her methods to cook up something new, completely on our own. This blending of ancient formulas and personal methods represents what Ms. Wolfe calls Aquarian Shamanism.

In the Shadow of the Shaman is designed to communicate in the most practical, direct ways possible, so that the wisdom and the energy may be shared for the benefits of all. Whatever your system or tradition, you will find this to be a valuable book, a resource, a friend, a gentle guide, and support on your journey. Dancing in the shadow of the shaman, you will find new dimensions of Spirit.

0-87542-888-6, 384 pp., 6 x 9, illus. **$14.95**

CELTIC MYTH & MAGIC
HARNESS THE POWER OF THE
GODS & GODDESSES
Edain McCoy

Tap into the mythic power of the Celtic goddesses, gods, heroes, and heroines to aid your spiritual quests and magickal goals. *Celtic Myth & Magic* explains how to use creative ritual and pathworking to align yourself with the energy of these archetypes, whose potent images live deep within your psyche.

Celtic Myth & Magic begins with an overview of forty-nine different types of Celtic Paganism followed today, then gives specific instructions for evoking and invoking the energy of the Celtic pantheon to channel it toward magickal and spiritual goals and into esbat, sabbat, and life-transition rituals. Three detailed pathworking texts will take you on an inner journey where you'll join forces with the archetypal images of Cuchulain, Queen Maeve, and Merlin the Magician to bring their energies directly into your life. The last half of the book clearly details the energies of over three hundred Celtic deities and mythic figures so you can evoke or invoke the appropriate deity to attain a specific goal.

This inspiring, well-researched book will help solitary Pagans who seek to expand the boundaries of their practice to form working partnerships with the divine.

1–56718–661–0, 7 x 10, 464 pp., softbound $19.95

To order, call 1-800-THE MOON
Prices subject to change without notice